*The*
MYSTERY OF ATLANTIS

# The
# MYSTERY
## of
# ATLANTIS

*Charles Berlitz*

SOUVENIR PRESS

Copyright © 1969, 1975 by Charles Berlitz

The right of Charles Berlitz to be identified as author
of this work has been asserted by him in accordance with
the Copyright, Designs and Patents Act 1988.

First published in the USA by
Grosset & Dunlap

First British edition published 1976 by
Souvenir Press Ltd.,
43 Great Russell Street, London WC1B 3PA

Reprinted 1976 (twice)
Reissued in paperback 1996
Reprinted 2001

All rights reserved. No part of this publication
may be reproduced, stored in a retrieval system,
or transmitted, in any form or by any means, electronic,
mechanical, photocopying, recording or otherwise, without
the prior permission of the Copyright owner.

ISBN 0 285 62211 0 (casebound)
ISBN 0 285 63351 1 (paperback)

Printed in Great Britain by
The Guernsey Press Company Ltd., Guernsey, Channel Islands

# Contents

# Foreword

As mankind rushes headlong into the future and into limitless space, his horizons have also expanded *backward*. He has become increasingly interested in his own past. The boundaries of early civilization have been pushed backward with each year. And as new discoveries are made and new carbon 14 readings (which help to determine the age of certain artifacts) are taken, it appears that man was civilized, in varying degrees, thousands of years before the period we have customarily assumed, and not always in the favorite spots we have usually considered—such as the Fertile Crescent of the Middle East.

Where then was the first civilization? Were the other early civilizations "exported" from a central point? Was there an older, wiser culture that helped to form Egypt, Sumeria, Crete, Etruria, the Mediterranean Islands and adjacent shores, and even influenced the cultures of the Americas?

To these questions there comes a faint but pervasive answer, a word that seems to echo from an uncertain past, a word like a name called over a misty ocean. The word is—Atlantis. To many Atlantis is the lost Atlantic continent, the first home of civilization, a fair and golden land struck down by a series of convulsions at the height of its power and now lying deep under the ocean, with only the tops of its mountains protruding from the ocean floor.

To others Atlantis is merely a legend, invented by Plato, the Greek philosopher, as a background for two of his dialogues, and maintained in popular fancy by other romanticists throughout the centuries. To still others, Atlantis was a true precursor of the early civilizations, documented, as it was, in early though incomplete records, but located somewhere other than in the Atlantic—and each projected location has its numerous partisans.

If we consult the encyclopedia we will find that Atlantis is considered "a legend." It does not fit into recorded history. Geologists and oceanographers however, agree that something like a continent once did exist in the Atlantic but they hesitate to locate it within the scope of civilized mankind.

But Atlantis is still with us, and now more than ever. It has remained a part of our culture whether we believe in it or not. It has been the subject of over 5,000 books, it has inspired classics, it has influenced history and even contributed to the discovery of the New World.

Every time an undersea city or culture is located, and there are and will be many because of the gradual rise of the world's water level, as well as the sinking of some sections of coast line, the magic word—Atlantis—springs to the lips of the discoverer. Within the last year Atlantis has been "discovered" in the island of Thera in the Mediterranean, which lost portions of its land to the sea in ancient volcanic convulsions.

Conversely the remarkable readings of Edgar Cayce predicted that in 1968 or '69 an Atlantean temple would arise near Bimini, in the Bahamas. Several underwater structures have actually been sighted nearby, and at this writing are now under investigation.

The "legend" of Atlantis it can be so called, is at least a very lively one, and constantly self-renewing, like another well-known legend, that of the phoenix. As each generation learns of this great folk memory—the lost continent, or lost paradise, at the bottom of the sea—new questions are asked and new explanations are offered. And, with present day research equipment, the moment may be at hand for the solution of this ancient enigma and for reassessing the age of civilized man as well as the location of his first great civilization.

# 1 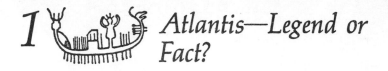 Atlantis—Legend or Fact?

Atlantis is the world's greatest mystery story. Its very name evokes a mysterious sense of familiarity and lost memories, as well it should, for our ancestors have been making conjectures about Atlantis for thousands of years.

If you look up Atlantis in an encyclopedia you will find it listed as a "mythical" lost continent and, among other annotations, that it was described by Plato in the 4th century B.C. in two of his dialogues, *Timaeus* and *Critias*. The content of these dialogues concerns a visit by Solon to Egypt wherein he learned that the Egyptian priests in Sais had written records about "an island continent beyond the Pillars of Hercules (the ancient name for Gibraltar) called Atlantis, the heart of a great and wonderful empire" possessing a large population, golden roofed cities, mighty fleets and armies for invasion and conquest.

In his description of Atlantis Plato mentioned that "the island was larger than Libya and Asia put together (Libya apparently meaning the then known part of Africa) and from the island you might pass through to the opposite continent which surrounded the true ocean. . . ." Plato described Atlantis as an earthly paradise, a combination of mighty mountains, fertile plains, navigable rivers, rich mineral deposits and a large and thriving population. This mighty empire "in a single day and night disappeared beneath the sea."

The date of its sinking, as calculated by Plato, was about 9,000 years before his time, which would make the time of its submergence about 11,500 years ago. Plato's reference to this lost continent, which will be discussed more fully in Chapter 3, was alternately doubted and believed through the centuries. Part of his story was certainly vindicated by the eventual discovery of the "opposite continent" in 1492. As more becomes known about the ocean bottom and as the limits of mankind's pre-history are pushed backwards in time, it may mean that other points of Plato's story will be recognized as equally true.

Whether true or not, and whatever the psychological implications may be, a great surge of race memory points to somewhere in the Atlantic as the original tribal or racial home or an earthly paradise where souls go after death.

If Atlantis had existed the tribes and races of people of the perimeter *on both sides of the Atlantic* would remember it or at least possess some reference to it in tribal memory or written records. A curious coincidence in names should be noted in this regard. The Welsh and ancient English pointed to the western ocean for their earthly paradise, which they called *Avalon*. The ancient Greeks situated the island beyond the Pillars of Hercules and called it *Atlantis*. The Babylonians placed their paradise in the western ocean and referred to it as *Aralu*, while the Egyptians situated their abode of souls "far to the west in the middle of the ocean" and called it, among other names, *Aaru* or *Aalu* as well as *Amenti*. The Celtic tribes of Spain and also the Basques preserve traditions of their homeland in the western ocean; and the original Gauls of France, especially those in the western sections, had the tradition that their ancestors came from the middle of the western ocean as a result of a catastrophe which destroyed their homeland. Ancient tribes of Africa held traditions of a western continent, referring to tribes called the *Atarantes* and the *Atlantioi*, a dried up sea called *Attala* and, of course, the *Atlas* Mountains. In the Canary Islands (in theory themselves the mountain tops of Atlantis) a series of ancient caverns are called *Atalaya*, whose inhabitants, even in Roman times, were reported to retain memories of the sinking of Atlantis. The Arabs believed that the people of *Ad* lived before the great flood and were destroyed by the flood as punishment for their sins. And what of our own Judeo-Christian traditions? Could Adam (Ad-am) be a reference, not to the first man, but to the first race?

In North and South America we find a series of extraordinary coincidences. The majority of Indian tribes have legends telling that they came from the east or obtained the arts of civilization from super-men who came from an eastern continent. The Aztec people preserved the name of the land of their origin—Aztlán, in fact the name Aztec is itself derived from Aztlán. In the Aztec language (Nahuatl) *atl* means "water" and this same word has the same meaning in the Berber language of North Africa. Quetzalcoatl, the god of the Aztecs and other Mexican peoples was said to be a white, bearded man, who came to the Valley of Mexico from the ocean and, after his civilizing mission, returned to Tlapallan. The Quiche Maya, in their sacred book, refer to the eastern country where they once lived as a true paradise, "where whites and blacks lived in peace" until the god Hurakan (Hurricane) became angry and flooded the earth. When the Spanish conquerors first explored Venezuela they found a settlement called Atlán, peopled by white Indians (or so they appeared to the Spaniards) who said their ancestors had been among the survivors of a drowned land.

Among all these linguistic coincidences perhaps the most striking is our own. The very name of the ocean—the Atlantic—that we swim in, fly or sail over, may be a link to the legend of ancient golden cities lying on the ocean bottom. Of course, the name Atlantic comes from Atlas, the giant of Greek legend who supported the sky. But was not the story of Atlas itself an allegory of power, perhaps the power of the Atlantean empire? In Greek, Atlantis means "daughter of Atlas."

Legends of a great flood and the disappearance of an advanced civilization are common to almost all races, nations and tribes with written records or oral traditions. It has been suggested that the similarity of our own biblical records of the Flood and those of Sumeria, Babylonia, Assyria and Persia as well as the other ancient Mediterranean nations may stem from memories of a great flood in the Middle East. But would this also explain the flood legends of Scandinavia, China, India and a great majority of the Indian tribes of the New World in both North and South America?

These legends of a great flood, with the recurring mention of survivors who started a new world on the ruins of the old are held throughout the world and apparently refer to something which actually happened. Certainly it must be considered that, if the earth were covered by water alone, the waters would not have receded, as they would have had no place to go. Therefore one may assume that the great flood, as remembered by its survivors, referred to a special inundation with accompanying rain and climatic disturbances during which it appeared, to the survivors at least, that the whole world was underwater. It is this memory of a flood and a common memory of an earthly paradise, usually located on a fertile and beautiful island in the middle of the Atlantic, as well as the many references by classical writers to such an island, that has fascinated men through the ages and certainly influenced the discovery and conquest of America.

Critics of the Atlantean theory have argued that there should be more references from antiquity to Atlantis than those which we have (and which we will later examine). However, considering the state of ancient records and pending the possible discovery of new ones, one might consider it unusual that we have as much as we do. We actually know that some records of Atlantis were lost because several of the references we have refer to more complete records that have since been lost. For, besides the general destruction of Greek and Roman manuscripts through the barbarian invasions, a great deal of classical literature was systematically destroyed, sometimes by the very people who inherited it. Pope Gregory, for example, ordered classical literature destroyed "lest it distract the faithful from the contemplation of heaven." Amru, the Moslem conqueror of Alexandria, where the greatest library of antiquity, more than a million volumes, was located, used the classical book rolls as a six month's supply of fuel to heat the city's 4,000 public baths on the grounds that, if the ancient books contained information which was in the Koran it was superfluous and, if the information contained in the books was not in the Koran it was of no use to true believers. No one knows what references to Atlantis may have gone into heating bath water for the Arab conquerors, as Alexandria was a scientific as well as a literary center. The Spanish conquerors of the New World continued this destruction of an-

cient records when Bishop Landa destroyed all the Mayan writings
he could find in Yucatan with the exception of about six now in
European museums. The Maya, with their direct reference to their
origin and surprising scientific knowledge, might have provided
valuable information about the lost continent, and still may, if new
records are discovered.

If ancient writings have been lost, modern works on Atlantis are
not lacking. About 5,000 books and pamphlets have been published in the world's leading languages, mostly within the last 150
years. The very number of books on this subject demonstrates the
appeal that the mystery of Atlantis holds over man's imagination.
In fact, a group of English newspapermen once voted the re-emergence of Atlantis the fourth most important news story they could
imagine, several places ahead of the second coming of Christ!

Among the thousands of books written in the past century and
a half a passage in a book by Ignatius Donnelly deserves to be cited
as typical in essence of the firm belief held by so many in the actual
existence of an Atlantean continent, the origin of civilization.
Donnelly offered thirteen propositions at the beginning of his book
on Atlantis published in 1882 which are still distinguished by their
verve, originality and above all by their tone of definite certainty.
The propositions are:

1. That there once existed in the Atlantic Ocean, opposite the
mouth of the Mediterranean Sea, a large island, which was the
remnant of an Atlantic Continent, and known to the ancient
world as Atlantis.

2. That the description of this island given by Plato is not, as
has long been supposed, fable, but veritable history.

3. That Atlantis was the region where man first rose from a
state of barbarism to civilization.

4. That it became, in the course of ages, a populous and mighty nation, from whose overflowings the shores of the Gulf of Mexico, the Mississippi River, the Amazon, the Pacific coast of South America, the Mediterranean the west coast of Europe and Africa, the Baltic, the Black Sea, and the Caspian were populated by civilized nations.

5. That it was the true Antediluvian world; the Garden of Eden; the Gardens of the Hesperides; the Elysian Fields; the Gardens of Alcinous; . . . the Olympos; the Asgard of the traditions of the ancient nations; representing a universal memory of a great land, where early mankind dwelt for ages in peace and happiness.

6. That the gods and goddesses of the ancient Greeks, the Phoenicians, the Hindus and the Scandinavians were simply the kings, queens and heroes of Atlantis; and the acts attributed to them in mythology are a confused recollection of real historic events.

7. That the mythology of Egypt and Peru represented the original religion of Atlantis, which was sun-worship.

8. That the oldest colony formed by the Atlanteans was probably in Egypt, whose civilization was a reproduction of that of the Atlantic island.

9. That the implements of the "Bronze Age" of Europe were derived from Atlantis. The Atlanteans were also the first manufacturers of iron.

10. That the Phoenician alphabet, parent of all the European alphabets, was derived from an Atlantean alphabet. . . .

11. That Atlantis was the original seat of the Aryan or Indo-European family of nations, as well as of the Semetic peoples, and possibly also of the Turanian races.

12. That Atlantis perished in a terrible convulsion of nature, in which the whole island sunk into the ocean, with nearly all its inhabitants.

13. That a few persons escaped in ships and on rafts, and carried to the nations east and west tidings of the appalling catastrophe, which has survived to our own time in the Flood and Deluge legends of the different nations of the old and new worlds.

Donnelly's book and thousands that followed may be said to have started an Atlantis "movement" which has persisted, with varying intensity, to the present day. Writers and students have engaged in reexamination of the ancient texts still available on the subject and have conscientiously studied classic myths, indigenous legends, and indications bearing on the subject to be found in such varied fields as biology, anthropology, geology, botany, linguistics and seismology. The material is vast and the results are subject to interpretation.

The first five of these disciplines furnish, according to interpretation, a vast amount of information indicating that a land bridge once connected the new world and the old. This may have been first a land connection, then a large continent which was finally broken up into a series of separated islands. This would not only explain unusual parallels in these sciences but even the culture patterns and common myths. And, with regard to seismology, the Atlantic is one of the least stable parts of the world's crust and is subject to upheavals along the whole submarine Northern Mid-Atlantic Ridge, which extends along the sea bottom from Northern Brazil to Iceland, and whose upheavals can still cause raising or lowering of land masses. Recent developments in science, new techniques in archeological dating, revolutionary conclusions re-

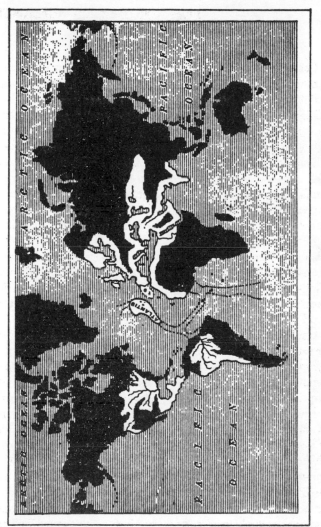

Atlantean "colonial" spread over the world, as envisioned by Donnelly.

garding the age of civilized man and, above all, the increasing scope and depth of underwater exploration has prepared a field for new discoveries. In fact, some of these may already have been made, but have not yet been assessed.

Prior to the dating, locating, excavating and underwater exploration techniques that we now have at our disposal, theorists and researchers on Atlantis had reached a point in traditional fields of investigation beyond which they could not go. At present the area and means of investigation has considerably widened in scope.

# 2 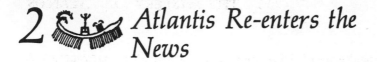 Atlantis Re-enters the News

Atlantis is still making news. In the past several years it has been "re-discovered" twice! Once in the Mediterranean, and across the Atlantic an Atlantean temple is said to be rising to the surface off Bimini, in the Bahamas. The reason the underwater building has been referred to in the press as an Atlantean temple is because of the striking coincidence of the prediction, twenty-eight years ago, by Edgar Cayce, who stated in 1940 that an Atlantean temple would rise out of the waters off Bimini in 1968 or '69.

Edgar Cayce, the psychic researcher and ESP investigator, of Virginia Beach, Virginia, had previously given, through the period from 1923 to 1944, many psychic "readings," or interviews, about Atlantis, life in Atlantis and land changes in general. These interviews, though numerous, represent only a part of his many psychic readings and predictions which have resulted in the establishment of a foundation bearing his name as well as an association with branches in numerous American cities.

In describing Atlantis he reported that part of sunken Atlantis was located under the ocean near the Bahamas and, specifically, that the Bahamas themselves were the peaks of the sunken island of Poseidia, part of the "western section of Atlantis." In 1940 Cayce gave the date of 1968 or '69 for the re-emergence of part of Atlantis, the part near Bimini, saying: "Poseidia will be among the first portions of Atlantis to rise again. Expected in '68 and '69. Not so far away!"

By a curious coincidence several buildings seem to be coming to the surface off Bimini, as well as at the northern tip of Andros. What they are and how old they are has not yet been established. However, the most striking point about their appearance is that these mysterious underwater buildings have appeared in the exact location that Cayce, in 1940, predicted that they would appear!

The underwater buildings were sighted and photographed from the air by two commercial pilots, one of whom, as he was a member of the Cayce Foundation, was actually looking for them, while flying his regular assignments, since he was aware that the re-emergence of Atlantean buildings had been predicted. It is interesting to note that the airplane for many years has been a remarkable aid to archeologists as, depending on the visibility and calmness of the water, it has been possible to discover and photograph from the air numerous ancient harbors, fortifications and cities.

South of this point there is a deep called Tongue of the Ocean at a depth of about 18,000 feet, a point which fits in nicely with Cayce's "reading" that the former Atlantean lands off Bimini are the highest point of a sunken continent. Preliminary underwater investigation has indicated that the building is constructed on bedrock and that the walls have been covered by sand, making it difficult to see from underwater, but easy from the air, from where the rectangular features of the building are more evident. Since the buildings are now so close to the surface, measures have had to be taken to protect them from treasure hunters who are less interested in establishing their antiquity than in the possibility of plunder.

Other underwater ruins have subsequently been found near other Caribbean Islands, including what appears to be an entire city submerged off the coast of Haiti, and still another at the bottom of a lake. What appears to be an underwater road (or perhaps a series of plazas or foundations) was discovered in 1968 off north Bimini beneath several fathoms of water. From these numerous findings, it would appear that part of the continental shelf of the Atlantic and Carribbean was once dry land, sunk or flooded during a period when man was already civilized.

The emerging underwater buildings off Bimini and Andros are being presently studied to determine whether they were part of a Mayan culture complex or the even earlier one predicted by Cayce. If their Mayan origin is established, this would still in itself not necessarily detract from the Atlantean theory, since the Mayas themselves are considered by many to be, if not the descendants of survivors of Atlantis, at least people brought to their relatively high level of civilization by the Atlanteans—an ancient version of help to "underdeveloped nations."

An expedition to the island of Thera, located in the Aegean directly north of Crete, has focused considerable attention on the theory that Thera itself, which apparently was blown apart in 1500 B.C. with the resultant submergence of a large land area, was the actual disaster that furnished Plato with the report of the destruction of a continent. It is known that a mysterious disaster struck the advanced Cretan civilization at about the same time.

Previously the Cretan empire was more culturally advanced

than the empires which followed it, possessing even running water and bathroom facilities of surprising modernity, tinted glass goblets, glazed dinner services and elaborate and revealing styles in dress.

In ancient times Thera was also called Stronghyli, meaning "the rotunda," but after its explosion the northwestern part of the island was blown away and sunk beneath the sea, leaving the island in the shape of a crescent. This explosion and connected volcanic shocks as well as tidal waves caused by seismic disturbances may have been one of the reasons for Crete's decline and eventual conquest by the Achaean Greeks.

However, numerous volcanic eruptions through the centuries in the Mediterranean do not preclude a greater one, as reported by Plato, beyond the Pillars of Hercules. The interesting point is that as soon as any submerged lands with connected archaic cultures are found, and there will be constantly more with new underwater exploration techniques, the question is posed—"Is this the lost Atlantis of legend?"

For Atlantis, the world's oldest civilization or legend, according to one's point of view, has never ceased to haunt the consciousness of mankind, evidenced by the thousands of books and tracts written and still appearing on a subject whose existence has yet to be definitely established. And still this legend or race memory is considered newsworthy today!

It is almost as if, realizing that there now exist improved methods of archeological investigation, modern man expects to receive confirmation of his own lost past and is waiting for modern science to fill him in on the gaps in the common family history.

Even as this book goes to press several others dealing with Atlantis or the Thera explanation of Atlantis have already appeared or are being published as well as new reprints of books written many years ago but still pertinent and informative. Over the past few years a popular song by Donovan still echoes public interest in Atlantis, with its implied reaching back for knowledge of our past and the golden age of man.

# 3 ᗧᗧᗧᗧ The Mystery of Atlantis

Atlantis is history's greatest mystery story. The most complete of the ancient records of Atlantis, the *Timaeus* and *Critias* dialogues of Plato, are presented as a record of events which Solon of Athens learned from Egyptian priests at Sais, and are a mystery in themselves. Did Plato write these dialogues to illustrate the idea of a perfect state, or as pro-Athenian propaganda? In any event the descriptions of Atlantis are detailed and the most complete available from ancient records, unless the Egyptian records, if they exist, can be found. In addition to which Plato was not given to discussing fables, but specialized in philosophy and took special pains to these dialogues to repeat that they were not fiction but fact.

Plato first discussed Atlantis in the dialogue known as *Timaeus*:

CRITIAS: "Then listen, Socrates, to a strange tale, which is, however, certainly true, as Solon, who was the wisest of the seven sages, declared . . . that there were of old great and marvellous actions of the Athenians, which have passed into oblivion through time and the destruction of the human race—and one, in particular, which was the greatest of them all, the recital of which will be a suitable testimony of our gratitude to you. . . ."

SOCRATES: "Very good; and what is this ancient famous action of which Critias spoke, not as a mere legend, but as a veritable action of the Athenian state, which Solon recounted?"

CRITIAS: ". . . If Solon had only, like other poets, made poetry the business of his life, and had completed the tale which he brought with him from Egypt, and had not been compelled, by reasons of the factions and troubles which he found stirring in this country when he came home, to attend to other matters, in my opinion he would have been as famous as Homer, or Hesiod, or any poet."

SOCRATES: "And what was that poem about, Critias?"

CRITIAS: "About the greatest action which the Athenians ever did, and which ought to have been most famous, but which, through the lapse of time and the destruction of the actors, has not come down to us."

SOCRATES: "Tell us the whole story, and how and from whom Solon heard this veritable tradition."

CRITIAS: "At the head of the Egyptian Delta, where the river Nile divides, there is a certain district which is called the district of Sais, and the great city of the district is also called Sais, and is the city from which Amasis the king was sprung. And the citizens have a diety who is their foundress: she is called in the Egyptian tongue Neith, which is asserted by them to be the same whom the Hellenes called Athene. Now, the citizens of this city are great lovers of the Athenians, and say that they are in some way related to them. Thither came Solon, who was received by them with great honor; and he asked the priests, who were most skilful in such matters, about antiquity, and made the discovery that neither he nor any other Hellene knew anything worth mentioning about the times of old. On one occasion, when he was drawing them on to speak of antiquity, he began to tell about the most ancient things in our part of the world—about Phoroneus, who is called 'the first,' and about Niobe; and, after the Deluge, to tell of the lives of Deucalion and Pyrrha; and he traced the genealogy of their descendants, and attempted to reckon how many years old were the events of which he was speaking, and to give the dates. Thereupon, one of the priests, who was of very great age, said, 'O Solon, Solon, you Hellenes are but children, and there is never an old man who is an Hellene.' Solon, hearing this, said, 'What do you mean?' 'I mean to say,' he replied, 'that in mind you are all young; there is no old opinion handed down among you by ancient tradition, nor any science which is hoary with age. And I will tell you the reason of this; there have been, and there will be again, many destructions of mankind arising out of many causes. There is a story which even you have preserved, that once upon a time Phaëthon, the son of Helios, having yoked the steeds in his father's chariot, because he was not able to drive them in the path of his father, burnt up all there was upon the earth, and was himself destroyed by a thunderbolt. Now, this has the form of a myth, but really signifies a declination of the bodies moving around the earth and in the heavens, and a great conflagration of things upon the earth recurring at long intervals of time: when this happens, those who live upon the mountains and in dry and lofty places are more liable to destruction than those who dwell by rivers or on the sea-shore; and from this calamity the Nile, who is our never-failing savior, saves and delivers us. When, on the other hand, the gods purge the earth with a deluge of water, among you herdsmen and shepherds on the mountains are the survivors, whereas those of you who live in cities are carried by the rivers into the sea; but in this country neither at that time nor at any other does the water come from above on the fields, having always a tendency to come up from below, for which reason the things preserved here are said to be the oldest. The fact is, that whatever the extremity of winter frost or of summer sun does not prevent, the human race is always increasing at times, and at other times diminishing in numbers. And whatever happened either in your country or in ours, or in any other region of which we are informed—if any action which is noble or great, or in any other way remarkable has taken place, all that has been written down of old, and is preserved in our temples; whereas you and other nations are just being provided with letters and the other things which States require; and then, at the usual period, the stream from heaven descends like a pestilence, and leaves only those of you who are destitute of letters and education; and thus you have to begin all over again as children, and know nothing of what happened in ancient times, either among us or among yourselves. As for those genealogies of yours which you have recounted to us, Solon, they are no better than the tales of children; for, in the first place, you remember one deluge only, whereas there were many of them; and, in the next place, you do not know that there dwelt in your land the fairest and noblest race of men which ever lived, of whom you and your whole city are but a seed or remnant. And this was unknown to you, because for many generations the survivors of that destruction died and made no sign. For there was a time, Solon, before that great deluge of all, when the city which now is Athens was first in war, and was pre-eminent for the excellence of her laws, and is said to have performed the noblest deeds, and to have had the fairest constitution of any of which tradition tells, under the face of heaven.' Solon marvelled at this, and earnestly requested the priest to inform him exactly and in order about these former citizens. 'You are welcome to hear about them, Solon,' said the priest, 'both for your own sake and that of the city; and, above all, for the sake of the goddess who is the common patron and protector and educator of both our cities. She founded your city a thousand years before ours, receiving from the earth and Hephaestus the seed of your race, and then she founded ours, the constitution of which is set down in our sacred registers as 8000 years old. As touching the citizens of 9000 years ago, I will briefly inform you of their laws and of the noblest of their actions; and the exact particulars of the whole we will hereafter go through at our leisure in the sacred registers themselves. If you compare these very laws with your own, you will find that many of ours are the counterpart of yours, as they were in the olden time. . . . "Many great and wonderful deeds are recorded of your State in our histories; but one of them exceeds all the rest in greatness and valor; for these histories tell of a mighty power which was aggressing wantonly against the whole of Europe and Asia, and to which your city put an end. This power came forth out of the Atlantic Ocean, for in those days the Atlantic was navigable; and there was an island situated in front of the straits which you call the Columns of Heracles: the island was larger than Libya and Asia put together, and was the way to other islands, and from the islands you might pass through the whole of the opposite continent which surrounded the true ocean; for this sea which is within the Straits of Heracles is only a harbor, having a narrow entrance, but that other is a real sea, and the surrounding land may be most truly called a continent. Now, in the island of Atlantis there was a great and wonderful empire, which had rule over the whole island and several others, as well as over part of the continent; and, besides these, they subjected the parts of Libya within the Columns of Heracles as far as Egypt, and of Europe as far as Tyrrhenia. The vast power thus gathered into one, endeavored to subdue at one blow our country and yours, and the whole of the land which was within the straits; and then, Solon, your country shone forth, in the excellence of her virtue and strength, among all mankind; for she was the first in courage and military skill, and was the leader of the Hellenes. And when the rest fell off from her, being compelled to stand alone, after having undergone the very extremity of danger, she defeated and triumphed over the invaders, and preserved from salvery those who were not yet subjected, and freely liberated all the others who dwelt within the limits of Heracles. But afterward there occurred violent earthquakes and floods, and in a single day and night of rain all your warlike men in a body sunk into the earth, and the island of Atlantis in like manner disappeared, and was sunk beneath the sea. And that is the reason why the sea in those parts is impassable and impenetrable, because there is such a quantity of shallow mud in the way; and this was caused by the subsidence of the island.' "

The following are excerpts from the second dialogue concerning Atlantis, called *Critias* or *The Atlantic*.

CRITIAS: "Let me begin by observing, first of all, that nine thousand was the sum of years which had elapsed since the war which was said to have taken place between all those who dwelt outside the Pillars of Heracles and those who dwelt within them: this war I am now to describe. Of the combatants on the one side the city of Athens was reported to have been the ruler, and to have directed

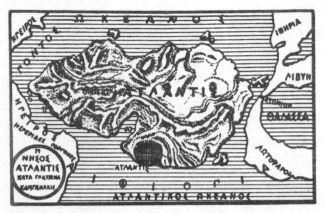

Suggested map of Atlantis by P. Kampanakis, a Greek researcher and writer and follower of the Platonian tradition of Atlantis. Spain is in the upper right hand corner, Europe is joined to Africa, and the Sahara Desert is represented as a sea, joined to the true ocean.

the contest; the combatants on the other side were led by the kings of the islands of Atlantis, which, as I was saying, once had an extent greater than that of Libya and Asia; and, when afterward sunk by an earthquake, became an impassable barrier of mud to voyagers sailing from hence to the ocean. The progress of the history will unfold the various tribes of barbarians and Hellenes which then existed, as they successively appear on the scene; but I must begin by describing, first of all, the Athenians as they were in that day, and their enemies who fought with them; and I shall have to tell of the power and form of government of both of them. Let us give the precedence to Athens . . .

"Many great deluges have taken place during the nine thousand years, for that is the number of years which have elapsed since the time of which I am speaking; and in all the ages and changes of things there has never been any settlement of the earth flowing down from the mountains, as in other places, which is worth speaking of; it has always been carried round in a circle, and disappeared in the depths below. The consequence is that, in comparison of what then was, there are remaining in small islets only the bones of the wasted body, as they may be called, all the richer and softer parts of the soil having fallen away, and the mere skeleton of the country being left. . . .

". . . . My great-grandfather, Dropidas, had the original writing, which is still in my possession, and was carefully studied by me when I was a child. . . .

"The tale, which was of great length, began as follows: I have before remarked, in speaking of the allotments of the gods, that they distributed the whole earth into portions differing in extent, and made themselves temples and sacrifices. And Poseidon, receiving for his lot Atlantis, begat children by a mortal woman, and settled them in a part of the island which I will proceed to describe. On the side toward the sea, and in the center of the whole island, there was a plain which is said to have been the fairest of all plains, and very fertile. Near the plain again, and also in the center of the island, at a distance of about fifty stadia, there was a mountain, not very high on any side. In this mountain there dwelt one of the earth-born primeval men of that country, whose name was Evenor, and he had a wife named Leucippe, and they had an only daughter, who was named Cleito. The maiden was growing up to womanhood when her father and mother died; Poseidon fell in love with her, and had intercourse with her; and, breaking the ground, enclosed the hill on which she dwelt all round, making alternate zones of sea and land, larger and smaller, encircling one another; there were two of land and three of water, which he turned as with a lathe out of the center of the island, equidistant every way, so that no man could get to the island, for ships and voyages were not yet heard of. He himself, as he was a god, found no difficulty in making special arrangements for the center island, bringing two streams of water under the earth, which he caused to ascend as springs, one of warm water and the other of cold, and making every variety of food to spring up abundantly in the earth. He also begat and brought up five pairs of male children, dividing the island of Atlantis into ten portions: he gave to the first-born of the eldest pair his mother's dwelling and the surrounding allotment, which was the largest and best, and made him king over the rest; the others he made princes, and gave them rule over many men and a large territory. And he named them all: the eldest, who was king, he named Atlas, and from him the whole island and the ocean received the name of Atlantic. To his twin brother, who was born after him, and obtained as his lot the extremity of the island toward the Pillars of Heracles, as far as the country which is still called the region of Gades in that part of the world, he gave the name which in the Hellenic language is Eumelus, in the language of the country which is named after him, Gadeirus. Of the second pair of twins, he called one Ampheres and the other Evaemon. To the third pair of twins he gave the name Mneseus to the elder, and Autochthon to the one who followed him. Of the fourth pair of twins he called the elder Elasippus and the younger Mestor. And to the fifth pair he gave to the elder the name of Azies and to the younger Diaprepes. All these and their descendants were the inhabitants and rulers of divers islands in the open sea; and also, as has been already said, they held sway in the other direction over the country within the Pillars as far as Egypt and Tyrrhenia. Now Atlas had a numerous and honorable family, and his eldest son handed on to his eldest for many generations; and they had such an amount of wealth as was never before possessed by kings and potentates, and is not likely ever to be again, and they were furnished with everything which they could have, both in city and country. For, because of the greatness of their empire, many things were brought to them from foreign countries, and the island itself provided much of what was required by them for the uses of life. In the first place, they dug out of the earth whatever was to be found there, mineral as well as metal, and that which is now only a name, and was then something more than a name—orichalcum—was dug out of the earth in many parts of the island, and, with the exception of gold, was esteemed the most precious of metals among the men of those days. There was an abundance of wood for carpenters' work, and sufficient maintainance for tame and wild animals. Moreover, there were a great number of elephants on the island, and there was provision for animals of every kind, both for those which live in lakes and marshes and rivers, and also for those which live on mountains and on plains, and therefore for the animal which is the largest and most voracious of them. Also, whatever fragrant things there are in the earth, whether roots, or herbage, or woods, or distilling drops of flowers or fruits, grew and thrived in that land; and again, the cultivated fruit of the earth, both the dry edible fruit and other species of food, which we call by the general name of legumes, and the fruits having a hard rind, affording drinks, and meats, and ointments, and good store of chestnuts and the like, which may be used to play with, and are fruits which spoil with keeping—and the pleasant kinds of dessert which console us after dinner, when we are full and tired of eating—all these that sacred island lying beneath the sun brought forth fair and wondrous in infinite abundance. All these things they received from the earth, and they employed themselves in constructing their temples, and palaces, and harbors, and docks; and they arranged the whole country in the following manner: First of all they bridged over the zones of sea which surrounded the ancient metropolis, and made a passage into and out of the royal palace; and then they began to build the palace in the habitation of the god and of their ancestors. This they continued to ornament in successive generations, every king surpassing the one who came before him to the utmost of his power, until they made the building a marvel to behold for size and for beauty. And, beginning from the sea, they dug a canal three hundred feet in width and one hundred feet in depth, and fifty stadia in length, which they carried through to the outermost zone, making a passage from the sea up to this, which became a harbor, and leaving an opening sufficient to enable the largest vessels to find ingress. Moreover, they divided the zones of land which parted the zones of sea, constructing bridges of such a width as would leave a passage from a single trireme to pass out of one into another, and roofed them over; and there was a way underneath for the ships, for the banks of the zones were raised considerably above the water. Now the largest of the zones into which a passage was cut from the sea was three stadia in breadth, and the zone of land which came next of equal breadth; but the next two, as well the zone of water as of land, were two stadia, and the one which surrounded the central island was a stadium only in width. The island on which the palace was situated had a diameter of five stadia. This, and the zones and the bridge, which was the sixth part of a stadium in width, they surrounded by a stone wall, on either side placing towers, and gates on the bridges where the sea passed in. The stone which was used in the work they quarried from underneath the center island and from underneath the zones, on the outer as well as the inner side. One kind of stone was white, another black, and a third red; and, as they quarried, they at the same time hollowed out rocks double within, having roofs formed out of the native rock. Some of their buildings were simple, but in others they put together different stones, which they intermingled for the sake of ornament, to be a natural source of delight. The entire circuit of the wall which went round the outermost one they covered with a coating of brass, and the circuit of the next wall they coated with tin, and the third, which encompassed the citadel, flashed with the red light of orichalcum. The palaces in the interior of the citadel were constructed in this wise: In the center was a holy temple dedicated to Cleito and Poseidon, which remained inaccessible, and was surrounded by an enclosure of gold; this was the spot in which they originally begat the race of the ten princes, and thither they annually brought the fruits of the earth in their season from all the ten portions and performed sacrifices to each of them. Here, too, was Poseidon's own temple, of a stadium in length and half a stadium in width, and of a proportionate height, having a sort of barbaric splendor. All the outside of the temple, with the exception of the pinnacles, they covered with silver, and the pinnacles with gold. In the interior of the temple the roof was of ivory, adorned everywhere with gold and silver and orichalcum; all the other parts of the walls and pillars and floor they lined with orichalcum. In the temple they placed statues of gold: there was the god himself standing in a chariot—the charioteer of six winged horses—and of such a size that he touched the roof of the building with his head; around him there were a hundred Nereids riding on dolphins, for such was thought to be the number of them in that day. There were also in the interior of the temple other images which had been dedicated by private individuals. And around the temple on the outside were placed statues of gold of all the ten kings and of their wives; and there were many other great offerings, both of kings and of private individuals, coming both from the city itself and the foreign cities over which they held sway. There was an altar, too, which in size and workmanship corresponded to the rest of the work, and there were palaces in like manner which answered to the greatness of the kingdom and the glory of the temple.

"In the next place they used fountains both of cold and hot springs; these were very abundant, and both kinds wonderfully adapted to use by reason of the sweetness and excellence of their waters. They constructed buildings about them, and planted suitable trees; also cisterns, some open to the heaven, others which they roofed over, to be used in winter as warm baths. There were the king's baths, and the baths of private persons, which were kept apart; also separate baths for women, and others again for horses and cattle, and to them they gave as much adornment as was suitable for them. The water which ran off they carried, some to the grove of Poseidon, where were growing all manner of trees of wonderful height and beauty, owing to the excellence of the soil; the remainder was carried by aquaducts which passed over the bridges to the outer circles; and there were many temples built and dedicated to many gods; also gardens and places of exercise, some for men and some set apart for horses, in both of the two islands formed by the zones; and in the center of the larger of the two there was a race course of a stadium in width, and in length allowed to extend all round the island, for horses to race in. Also there were guard houses at intervals for the body-guard, the more trusted of whom had their duties appointed to them in the lesser zone, which was nearer the Acropolis; while the most trusted of all had houses given to them within the citadel, and about the persons of the kings. The docks were full of triremes and naval stores, and all things were quite ready for use. Enough of the plan of the royal palace. Crossing the outer harbors, which were three in number, you would come to a wall which began at the sea and went all round: this was everywhere distant fifty stadia from the largest zone and harbor, and enclosed the whole, meeting at the mouth of the channel toward the sea. The entire area was densely crowded with habitations; and the canal and the largest of the harbors were full of vessels and merchants coming from all parts, who, from their numbers, kept up a multitudinous sound of human voices and din of all sorts night and day. I have repeated his descriptions of the city and the parts about the ancient palace nearly as he gave them, and now I must endeavor to describe the nature and arrangement of the rest of the country. The whole country was described as being very lofty and precipitous on the side of the sea, but the country immediately about and surrounding the city was a level plain, itself surrounded by mountains which descended toward the sea; it was smooth and even, but on an oblong shape, extending in one direction three thousand stadia, and going up the country from the sea through the center of the island two thousand stadia; the whole region of the island lies toward the south, and is sheltered from the north. The surrounding mountains he celebrated for their number and size and beauty, in which they exceeded all that are now to be seen anywhere; having in them also many wealthy inhabited villages, and rivers and lakes, and meadows supplying food enough for every animal, wild or tame, and wood of various sorts, abundant for every kind of work. I will now describe the plain, which had been cultivated during many ages by many generations of kings. It was rectangular, and for the most part, straight and oblong; and what it wanted of the straight line followed the line of the circular ditch. The depth and width and length of this ditch were incredible, and gave the impression that such a work, in addition to so many other works, could hardly have been wrought by the hand of man. But I must say what I have heard. It was excavated to the depth of a hundred feet, and its breadth was a stadium everywhere; it was carried round the whole of the plain, and was ten thousand stadia in length. It received the streams which came down from the mountains, and winding round the plain, and touching the city at various points, was there let off into the sea. From above, likewise, straight canals of a hundred feet in width were cut in the plain, and again let off into the ditch, toward the sea; these canals were at intervals of a hundred stadia, and by them they brought down the wood from the mountains to the city, and conveyed the fruits of the earth in ships, cutting transverse passages from one canal into another, and to the city. Twice in the year they gathered the fruits of the earth—in winter having the benefit of the rains, and in summer introducing the water of the canals. As to the population, each of the lots in the plain had an appointed chief of men who were fit for military service, and the size of the lot was to be a square of ten stadia each way, and the total number of all the lots was sixty thousand.

"And of the inhabitants of the mountains and of the rest of the country there was also a vast multitude having leaders, to whom they were assigned according to their dwellings and villages. The leader was required to furnish for war the sixth portion of a war-chariot so as to make up a total of ten thousand chariots; also two horses and riders upon them, and a light chariot without a seat, accompanied by a fighting man on foot carrying a small shield, and having a charioteer mounted to guide the horses; also, he was bound to furnish two heavy-armed men, two archers, two slingers, three stone-shooters, and three javelin men, who were skirmishers, and four sailors to make up a complement of twelve hundred ships. Such was the order of war in the royal city—that of the other nine governments was different in each of them, and would be wearisome to narrate. As to offices and honors, the following was the arrangement from the first: Each of the ten kings, in his own division and in his own city, had the absolute control of the citizens, and in many cases of the laws, punishing and slaying whomsoever he would.

"Now the relations of their governments to one another were regulated by the injunctions of Poseidon as the law had handed them down. These were inscribed by the first men on a column of orichalcum, which was situated in the middle of the island, at the temple of Poseidon, whither the people were gathered together every fifth and sixth years alternately, thus giving equal honor to the odd and to the even number. And when they were gathered together they consulted about public affairs, and inquired if anyone had transgressed in anything, and passed judgement on him accordingly—and before they passed judgement they gave their pledges to one another in this wise: There were bulls who had the range of the temple of Poseidon; and the ten who were left alone in the temple, after they had offered prayers to the gods that they might take the sacrifices which were acceptable to them, hunted the bulls without weapons, but with staves and nooses; and the bull which they caught they led up to the column; the victim was then struck on the head by them, and slain over the sacred inscription. Now on

the column, besides the law, there was inscribed an oath invoking
mighty curses on the disobedient. When therefore, after offering
sacrifice according to their customs, they had burnt the limbs of
the bull, they mingled a cup and cast in a clot of blood for each of
them; the rest of the victim they took to the fire, after having made
a purification of the column all round. Then they drew from the
cup in golden vessels, and, pouring a libation on the fire, they swore
that they would judge according to the laws on the column, and
would punish anyone who had previously transgressed, and that for
the future they would not, if they could help, transgress any of the
inscriptions, and would not command or obey any ruler who com-
manded them to act otherwise than according to the laws of their
father Poseidon. This was the prayer which each of them offered
up for himself and for his family, at the same time drinking, and
dedicating the vessel in the temple of the god; and, after spending
some necessary time at supper, when darkness came on and the fire
about the sacrifice was cool, all of them put on most beautiful
azure robes, and, sitting on the ground at night near the embers of
the sacrifices on which they had sworn, and extinguishing all the
fire about the temple, they received and gave judgement, if any of
them had any accusation to bring against any one; and, when they
had given judgement, at daybreak they wrote down their sentences
on a golden tablet, and deposited them as memorials with their
robes. There were many special laws which the several kings had
inscribed about the temples, but the most important was the
following: That they were not to take up arms against one another,
and they were all to come to the rescue if any one city attempted to
overthrow the royal house. Like their ancestors, they were to delib-
erate in common about war and other matters, giving the suprem-
acy to the family of Atlas; and the king was not to have the power

of life and death over any of his kinsmen, unless he had the assent of the majority of the ten kings.

"Such was the vast power which the god settled in the lost island of Atlantis; and this he afterward directed against our land on the following pretext, as traditions tell: For many generations, as long as the divine nature lasted in them, they were obedient to the laws, and well-affectioned toward the gods, who were their kinsmen; for they possessed true and in every way great spirits, practicing gentleness and wisdom in the various chances of life, and in their intercourse with one another. They despised everything but virtue, not caring for their present state of life, and thinking lightly on the possession of gold and other property, which seemed only a burden to them; neither were they intoxicated by luxury; nor did wealth deprive them of their self-control; but they were sober, and saw clearly that all these goods are increased by virtuous friendship with one another, and that by excessive zeal for them, and honor of them, the good of them is lost, and friendship perishes with them.

"By such reflections, and by the continuance in them of a divine nature, all that which we have described waxed and increased in them; but when this divine portion began to fade away in them, and became diluted too often, and with too much of the mortal admixture, and the human nature got the upper hand, then, they being unable to bear their fortune, became unseemly, and to him who had an eye to see, they began to appear base, and had lost the fairest of their precious gifts; but to those who had no eye to see the true happiness, they still appeared glorious and blessed at the very time when they were filled with unrighteous avarice and power. Zeus, the god of gods, who rules with law, and is able to see into such things, perceiving that an honorable race was in a most wretched state, and wanting to inflict punishment on them, that they might be chastened and improved, collected all the gods into his most holy habitation, which, being placed in the center of the world, sees all things that partake of generation. And when he had called them together he spoke as follows: . . ."

There is no record of Plato ever having finished the second dialogue about Atlantis or having written a third one, which he had announced but apparently never wrote, or, if he did, it has been lost. The poem *Atlantikos*, attributed to Solon, has also disappeared in the course of centuries.

Plato's account has been supported and attacked ever since he wrote it. Some commentators assert that not only Solon but later Plato himself visited Egypt and personally corroborated this information, as did also Krantor, one of Plato's students, and that all of them had "seen the evidence." In all events this writing of Plato has had considerable impact on man's thoughts through the centuries and still has today. Some critics of the Atlantis theory have suggested that Atlantis is only remembered because of Plato. However, considering the growing interest in the question through the centuries and today, might it not eventually, at least in popular conception, be the other way around?

Aristotle (384–322 B.C.), a former pupil of Plato, is on record as one of the earliest disbelievers in Atlantis, although he himself wrote of a large island in the Atlantic that the Cathaginians knew as *Antilia*.

Krantor (4th century B.C.), a follower of Plato, reported that he too had seen the columns on which was preserved the story of Atlantis as reported by Plato. Other ancient writers wrote of a continent in the Atlantic, sometimes with names other than Atlantis and sometimes calling it Poseidonis after Poseidon, the god of the sea and the lord of Atlantis.

Plutarch (46–120 A.D.) told of such a continent called Saturnia and of an island in the ocean called Ogygia about five days sail to the west of Britain. The name Ogygia is also spoken of by Homer as the island home of the nymph Calypso.

Marcelinus (330–395 A.D.), a Roman historian who wrote that the intelligentsia of Alexandria considered the destruction of Atlantis an historical fact, described a class of earthquakes "which suddenly, by a violent motion, opened up huge mouths and so swallowed up portions of the earth, as in the Atlantic sea, on the coast of Europe, a large island was swallowed up. . . ."

Proclus (410–485A.D.), a member of the neo-Platonic school, said that not far to the west of Europe there were some islands whose inhabitants still kept the memory of a larger island which once ruled them and which had been swallowed up by the sea. In commenting on Plato, he wrote ". . . that such and so great an island once existed, is evident from what is said by certain historians regarding the external sea. According to them, there were seven islands in that sea, in their times, sacred to Persephonë, and three others of great size, one of which was sacred to Pluto, one to Ammon, and one to Poseidon, this last being a thousand stadia in area. They also say that the inhabitants of this island sacred to Poseidon preserved the remembrance of their ancestors, and of the Atlantic island that existed there, and was truly wonderful; and which had for centuries dominated all the islands in the Atlantic Sea, and was also sacred to Poseidon. . . ."

Homer (8th century B.C.) in *The Odyssey* quotes the goddess Athena as saying: "Our father, son of Kronos, exalted ruler . . . my heart is torn for wise Odysseus, wretched man, who so long parted from his friends, lives sadly on a seagirt isle at the very navel of the sea. On this wooded isle dwells a goddess, daughter of crafty Atlas who knows the depth of every sea and keeps the tall pillars that separate earth and heaven. . . ."

The reference to Atlas and Kronos are especially interesting in connection with "the seagirt isle at the very navel of the sea." Homer further tells about the ship of Odysseus reaching "the boundary of the world, deep flowing Okeanos. There lie the lands and the city of the Kimmerioi, veiled in fog and cloud. . . ."

In the *Odyssey* Homer tells of Scheria, an island far in the ocean where the Phaecians ". . . dwell apart, afar on the unmeasured deep amid its waves—the most remote of men. . . ." He also describes the city of Alcinoüs, ascribing to it a profusion of wealth and magnificence which reminds one of Plato's description of Atlantis. Although the names are dissimilar this powerful island of Scheria is another indication of a memory of an island continent beyond the Pillars of Hercules in the western ocean.

Since, according to Plato, his basic information on Atlantis came from Egyptian records, one would imagine that more Egyptian papyrus records would make some reference to Atlantis. Certain references in Egyptian records have so been interpreted, such as "the reign of the gods" over Egypt for thousands of years before the first recorded Egyptian dynasties. In addition, an Egyptian priest and historian Manetho gives us the approximate time that the Egyptians changed their calendar system as occuring in the same period that Plato reported the sinking of Atlantis—11,500 years ago. Other "lost" Egyptian records are reported to have been held in Russia before the Revolution in the St. Petersburg museum.

An especially intriguing record was said to have recounted an expedition sent by a Pharaoh of the second dynasty to find out what had become of Atlantis and to discover if anything remained of it. This expedition is reported to have returned in five years with its mission understandably unaccomplished. Egyptian records also tell of invasions by "people of the sea," who came "from the ends of the world," and have illustrated them with monumental wall paintings which still can be seen at Medinet Habu.

Although most Egyptian book-scrolls must have been burned in the destruction of the library at Alexandria, perhaps further written material may still be buried in some unopened Egyptian tomb, in a good state of preservation because of Egypt's dry climate.

Herodotus (5th century B.C.), the ancient Greek historian, has left us several references to a name similar to Atlantis, as well as to a mysterious city in the Atlantic Ocean, which some have considered an Atlantean colony or a prototype of Atlantis itself. He wrote: "The first of the Greeks to perform long voyages" were aquainted with Iberia (Spain) and a city called Tartessos, ". . . beyond the Pillars of Hercules . . ." from which the first traders "made by the return voyage a profit more than any Greeks before their day. . . ." (This last has a curiously modern ring, bridging the millennium from remote antiquity to the merchant fleets of Niarchos and Onassis!)

At another point in his histories Herodotus speaks of a tribe called the Atarantes and also of still another tribe, the Atlantes, ". . . who take their name from a mountain called Atlas, very tapered and round; so lofty, moreover, that the top, it is said, cannot be seen, the clouds never quitting it, neither summer nor winter. . . ."

Herodotus was interested in ancient as well as contemporary history of the time and believed that the Atlantic was let into the

Mediterranean basin by an earthquake which broke a land bridge at Gibraltar. He also, on finding fossils of sea shells in the hills of Egypt, speculated on the possibility of past lands being sunk into the sea and present lands being former sea bottoms.

In *The Peloponnesian Wars* Thucydides, (460–400 B.C.) speaking of earthquakes, wrote: ". . . The sea at Orobiai in Euboia, retiring from what was then the line of the coast and rising in a great wave, covered a part of the city; and then subsided in some places, but in others the inundation was permanent, and what was formerly land is now sea. The people who could not escape to high ground perished. A similar inundation occurred in the neighborhood of Atalantë, an island on the coast of the Opuntian Locri. . . ."

A Greek historian, Timagenes (1st century B.C.), commenting on the inhabitants of ancient Gaul, makes mention of a story current with them that they had once been invaded by people from an island which sank. He further states that some of the Gauls themselves believed that they came from a remote land in the middle of the ocean.

A manuscript called *Concerning the World*, attributed to Aristotle, gives evidence of a belief in other continents as follows: ". . . but there are probably many other continents, separated from ours by the sea which we must cross to reach them, some larger and others smaller, but all invisible to us, except our own. For all the islands are in relation to our seas, so is the inhabited world in relation to the Atlantic, and so are many other continents in relation to the whole sea; for they are islands surrounded by the sea. . . ."

The following writing by Apollodoros (2nd century B.C.) in

*The Library* is unusual in its reference to the Pleiades: ". . . Atlas and Pleionë, daughter of Okeanos, had seven daughters called the Pleiades, born to them Kyllene in Arkadia, to wit: Alkyone, Kelaino, Elektra, Sterope, Taÿgete, and Maia. . . . And Poseidon had intercourse with two of them, first with Kelaino, by whom he had Lykos, whom Poseidon made to dwell on the Islands of the Blest, and second with Alkyone. . . ." In telling about the Islands of the Blest in the Atlantic sea, Plutarch speaks of gentle breezes, soft dews and inhabitants "who may enjoy all things without trouble or labor." The seasons "are temperate" and the transitions "so moderate that the firm belief prevails, even among the Barbarians, that this is the seat of the Blessed, and that these are the Elysian fields celebrated by Homer. . . ."

Diodoros Siculus (the Sicilian) (1st century B.C.) wrote in some detail about a war between the Amazons and a people called the Atlantioi. The Amazons in this case came from an island in the west called Hespera, which lay in the Tritonis Marsh, "near the ocean which surrounds the earth" and the mountain "called by the Greeks Atlas. . . ." He further states: ". . . The story is also told that the marsh Tritonis disappeared from sight in the course of an earthquake, when parts of it which lay towards the ocean were torn asunder. . . ."

Diodoros further quotes the myth of the Atlantioi: ". . . The kingdom was divided among he sons of Uranos, the most renowned of whom were Atlas and Kronos. Of these sons Atlas received as his part the regions on the coast of the ocean, and he not only gave the name of Atlantioi to his peoples but likewise called the greatest mountain in the land Atlas. They also said that he perfected the science of astrology and was the first to publish to mankind the doctrine of the sphere; and it was for this reason that the idea was held that the entire heavens were supported upon the shoulders of Atlas. . . ."

Diodoros details the daughters of Atlas as given by Apollodoros, relating that they ". . . lay with the most renowned heroes and gods and thus became the first ancestors of the larger part of the race of human beings. . . . These daughters were also distinguished for their chastity, and after their death attained to immortal honor among men, by whom they were both enthroned in the heavens and endowed with the appellation of Pleiades. . . ."

He further provides a pleasant description of the Atlantic island: ". . . For there lies out in the deep off Libya an island of considerable size, and situated as it is in the ocean it is distant from Libya a voyage of a number of days to the west. Its land is fruitful, much of it being mountainous and not a little being a level plain of surpassing beauty. Through it flow navigable rivers which are used for irrigation, and the island contains many parts planted with trees of every variety and gardens of great multitudes which are traversed by streams of sweet water; on it also are private villas of costly construction, and throughout the gardens banqueting houses have been constructed in a setting of flowers, and in them the inhabitants pass their time during the summer season. . . . There is also excellent hunting of every manner of beast and wild animal. . . .

"And, speaking generally, the climate of this island is altogether so mild that it produces in abundance the fruits of the trees and the other seasonal fruits of the year, so that it would appear that the island, because of its exceptional felicity, were a dwelling place of the gods and not of men. . . ."

Theopompos (4th century B.C.) records a conversation between King Midas and a certain Silenos, describing a large outer continent peopled by warlike tribes, one of which had essayed a conquest of the "civilized world." (The comparative value of this source is somewhat lessened by the mention that Silenos was a satyr, whom King Midas had caught by getting him drunk on Greek wine!)

Tertullian (160–240 A.D.) refers to the sinking of Atlantis in discussing the changes of the earth: ". . . which, even now, . . . undergoes local mutations . . . when among her islands Delos is no more . . . Samos a heap of sand. . . . When, in the Atlantic, the island equal in size to Libya or Asia is looked for in vain; when . . . the side of Italy, cut through in the center by the shivering shock of the Asiatic and the Tyrrhenian seas, leaves Sicily as its relics. . . ."

The reference to the opening of the Sicilian Straits is also commented on by Philo Judaeus, (20B.C.–A.D.40) who writes: "Consider how many districts on the mainland, not only such as were near the coast, but even such as were completely inland, have been swallowed up by the waters; and consider how great a proportion of land has become sea and is now sailed over by innumerable ships. Who is ignorant of that most sacred Sicilian strait, which in old times joined Sicily to the continent of Italy?"

He further cites three Greek cities lying on the sea bottom—Aigara, Boura and Helike. (Helike is now being searched for by modern archeological methods near the present city of Corinth), and tops it off with a reference to "the island of Alantes which as Plato said . . . in one day and one night was overwhelmed beneath the sea in consequence of an extraordinary earthquake and inundation."

A reference from an early Christian, Arnobius Afer, (3rd

century A.D.) complains by inference that the Christians were being blamed for everything as he plaintively asks: "Did we (Christians) bring it about, that 10,000 years ago a vast number of men burst forth from the island which is called the Atlantis of Neptune, as Plato tells us, and utterly ruined and blotted out countless tribes?"

Aelian (Claudius Aelianus [3rd century A.D.]) a classical writer, makes a rather unusual reference to Atlantis in his *The Nature of Animals*. In speaking of "rams of the sea" (thought to be seals), he says that they ". . . winter in the vicinity of the Strait which separates Corsica from Sardinia. . . . the male ram has around his forehead a white band. One would say it resembled the diadem of Lysimachus or Antigonus or some other Macedonian king. The inhabitants of the shores of the ocean tell that, in former times, the kings of Atlantis, descendants of Poseidon, wore on their heads, as a mark of power, the headband of the male rams, and that their wives, the queens, wore, as a sign of their power, headbands of the female rams. . . ."

This quotation from Aelian, coming down to us through the centuries, not as a description of Atlantis, but as an offhand note on headgear, gives a certain credence to a generally accepted belief in the former existence of Atlantis held in classical times.

What can one infer from these and other similar classical allusions? Although some of them seem to be mutually contradictory and although the names and the spellings change, there seem to be certain points in common. The ancient Mediterranean world believed that there were settled lands or a continent in the Atlantic and maintained somewhat confused memories about contact with them and also hostilities from raiding or expeditionary forces from such lands, and finally, a common tradition that the land or lands had sunk under the ocean.

Another Christian of antiquity, Kosmas Indikopleustes, (6th century A.D.) seems to anticipate by centuries the Russian claim "we invented it first" when he says that Plato ". . . expressed views similar to ours with modifications. . . . He mentions the ten generations as well as that land that lies beneath the ocean. And in a word it is evident that all of them borrow from Moses and publish his words as their own. . . ." Kosmas was apparently thinking of biblical references to the generations before the great flood which destroyed the people of the earth because of their wickedness. But the biblical reference to a flood is only a small part of a legend held in common by peoples in all parts of the world with the exception of Polynesia.

From the point of view of a modern investigator, therefore, the written evidence is not conclusive. But can it ever be so? We must remember the ancients were not writing for modern investigators and, in an age prior to memory banks, micro tapes, and even printing, had a completely different outlook on information and used gods and myths as a frame of reference for their writings. Proof of the existence of Atlantis must be sought in other sources as well as in the written commentaries of ancient writers.

# 4   Atlantis—The Persistent Memory

The tradition of the great flood, as contained in Genesis, is common to Babylonians, Assyrians, Persians, Egyptians, the city states of Asia Minor, Greece and Italy, and others around the Mediterranean and Caspian Seas and the Persian Gulf, and even India and China.

It would be plausible that stories of a great flood and the survival of people chosen by God or the gods to continue civilization by building a survival ship before the flood might be carried through Asia along the great caravan routes. To explain the similarity of the ancient Norse and Celtic legends would be somewhat more difficult. But how can one explain the fact that the American Indians of the New World had complete and analogous flood legends of their own, often referring to their being saved by coming to their new lands in ships from the East?

As we study flood legends, therefore, an unusual fact becomes apparent. *All* races seem to have the same story. It is conceivable that the Mediterranean peoples should conserve a tradition of a common disaster, but how would the Indians of the American continents know about it and have almost the identical legends?

According to the ancient Aztec picture-writing documents, for example, the Noah of the Mexican cataclysm was Coxcox, also called Teocipactli or Tezpi. He had saved himself and his wife in a boat or raft made of cypress wood. Paintings retracing the deluge of Coxcox have been discovered among the Aztecs, Miztecs, Zapotecs, Tlascalans and others. The tradition of the latter is still more strikingly in conformity with the story as we have it in Genesis, and in Chaldean sources. It tells how Tezpi embarked in a spacious vessel with his wife, his children and several animals, and grain, whose preservation was essential to the subsistence of the human race. When the great god Tezxatlipoca decreed that the waters should retire, Tezpi sent a vulture from the raft. The bird, feeding on the carcasses with which the earth was laden, did not return. Tezpi sent out other birds of which only the humming bird came back with a leafy branch in its beak. Then Tezpi, seeing that the country began to vegetate, left his raft on the mountain of Colhuacan.

The *Popul Vuh* was a Quiché Maya chronicle written in Mayan hieroglyphics. This was burned by the Spaniards at the time of the Conquest, but later transcribed from memory into Latin letters. This Mayan legend of the flood states: "Then the waters were agitated by the will of the Heart of Heaven (Hurakán), and a great inundation came upon the heads of these creatures. . . . They were engulfed, and a resinous thickness descended from heaven; . . . the face of the earth was obscured, and a heavy darkening rain commenced—rain by day and rain by night. . . . There was heard a great noise above their heads, as if produced by fire. Then were

men seen running, pushing each other, filled with despair; they
wished to climb upon their houses, and the houses, tumbling
down, fell to the ground; they wished to climb upon the trees, and
the trees shook them off; they wished to enter into the grottoes
(caves), and the grottoes closed themselves before them. . . .
Water and fire contributed to the universal ruin at the time of the
last great cataclysm which preceded the fourth creation."

Early explorers of North America were able to write down a
legend of Indian tribes around the Great Lakes: "In former times
the father of the Indian tribes dwelt *toward the rising sun.* Having
been warned in a dream that a deluge was coming upon the earth,
he built a raft, on which he saved himself, with his family and all
the animals. He floated thus for several months. The animals, who
at that time spoke, loudly complained and murmured against him.
At last a new earth appeared, on which he landed with all the
animals, who from that time lost the power of speech, as a punishment for their murmurs against their deliverer."

George Catlin, an early observer of the American Indians,
quotes a custom in which the principal participant is known as
"the only man" who "traveled" through the village, stopping in
front of each man's lodge, and crying until the owner of the lodge
came out and asked who he was, and what was the matter? To
which he replied by narrating 'the sad catastrophe which had happened on the earth's surface by the overflowing of the waters,'
saying that he was the 'only person saved from the universal calamity'; that he landed his big canoe on a high mountain in the west,
where he now resides; that he has come to open the medicine
lodge, which must needs receive a present of an edged tool from
the owner of every wigwam, that it may be sacrificed to the water;

for if this is not done there will be another flood, and no one will be saved, as it was with such tools that the big canoe was made.

A Hopi myth describes a land in which great cities were created and crafts flourished, but when the people became corrupt and warlike, a great flood destroyed the world. "Waves higher than mountains rolled in on the land and continents broke asunder and sank beneath the seas." The Iroquois tradition held that the world was once destroyed by water and only one family was saved, with two animals of each kind.

The Chibcha Indians, in Colombia, have a legend that the deluge was caused by the god Chibchacun whom Bochica, the civilizing teacher and principal god, punished by causing him in the future to bear the earth on his back. Earthquakes are said to be caused by Chibchacun shifting his balance. (In Greek legend Atlas bore the weight of the sky, and occasionally the world, on his shoulders.) And, in the Chibcha flood legend there is another remarkable parallel to the Greek flood legend. In order to get rid of the water that flooded the earth after the deluge Bochica opened a hole in the earth at Tequendama   a parallel to the flood waters in the Greek legend that disappeared through the orifice of Bambyce.

These flood legends are, in general, so close to our own that it is difficult to remember that they were current before the arrival of the white man in the New World. The Spanish invaders of Peru found that most of the people of the Inca empire believed that there had been a great flood which had killed all men except a few which the Creator had especially saved to repopulate the world.

An Inca legend about one such survivor mentions that he knew a flood was coming when he noticed his flocks of llamas kept looking sadly at the sky, and, warned by this, was able to climb a high mountain, where he and his family were safe from the ensuing flood. Another Inca legend mentions the length of rains as sixty days and sixty nights, which are twenty more than those mentioned in the Bible.

On the east coast of South America the Guarani Indians have a legend about Tamandere who, when the rains fell and began to cover the earth, stayed in the valley instead of going to the mountains with his companions. When the waters got higher he climbed up into a palm tree and ate fruit while he waited. As the waters rose the palm tree became uprooted and he and his wife rode on it while the land, the forest, and finally the mountains disappeared. God stopped the waters when they touched the sky, and Tamandere, who had now floated to the top of a mountain, descended when he heard the beating of wings of a heavenly bird as a signal that the waters were abating, and proceeded to repopulate the earth.

The Noahs of the Mediterranean, of Europe and of the Middle East, because of written records, are better known to us—such as Babylonian Ut-Napishtim, Baisbasbata, the flood survivor written of in the Hindu *Mahabarata,* Yima of Persian legend, and Deucalion of Greek mythology, who repopulated the earth by throwing stones, which became men. Apparently there was not just one Noah, but many, each, as far as the legend was concerned, unaware of the others.

The reason for the deluge in all these legends is almost always the same; mankind became wicked, and God decided to destroy them, but at the same time, to save one good couple or family to start over again.

This common memory of a great deluge would certainly be shared by people on both sides of the Atlantic if Atlantis had sunk in the catastrophe described by Plato, not only would the tides have risen throughout the world, but lowlands would be submerged, and storms, tempests, winds and earthquakes would lead an observer to believe that the world was truly coming to an end. And the seventh chapter of the Book of Genesis offers a particularly vivid report of the combination of rising waters and rain— "the same day were all the fountains of the great deep broken up, and the windows of heaven were opened . . ."

These shared legends of a great flood may perhaps refer to the sinking of Atlantis or the flooding of the Mediterranean or perhaps to both. Besides such common traditions, however, there is the matter of the name itself; that is, the names given to the earthly paradise or point of origin of the tribe or nation, especially striking in the traditions of the Indians of North and South America, as we have seen in the names Aztlán and Atlán, Tollán, and remarkable

Aztec representation of Aztlán, the original homeland, as depicted in a post-Conquest illustrated manuscript.

on the other side of the Atlantic in the resemblance of the names
of lost lands, such as Avalon, Lyonesse, Ys, Antilla, the Atlantic
island of the seven cities and, in the ancient Mediterranean, Atlantis, Atalanta, Atarant, Atlas, Aaru, Aalu and others which have
been detailed in Chapter I. All of these legends refer to a land sunk
beneath the sea.

It is interesting to consider that, even today, certain of these
races preserve traditions that they are descended from the Atlanteans or that their ancestors were culturally influenced by them.
This is especially true of the Basques of Northern Spain and South
Western France whose language has no connection with the other
European languages. Traditions about a western continent are still
held by the Berbers, whose language has certain points of similarity
to Basque.

Belief in the existence of Atlantis is widespread in Portugal,
Brazil and parts of Spain, which seems logical when one considers
that, if Atlantis had existed, the western part of the Iberian Peninsula would have been the part of Europe nearest to it.

One of the Catalan classics, published in 1878 consists of a long
poem called *La Atlántida*, by Jacinto Verdaguer—only one of
numerous literary creations by people who consider themselves
directly or indirectly descended from the Lost Continent.

There is a certain charm, for example, in reading in a present-
day Portuguese newspaper that the Chief of State has made a visit
to "*os vestígios da Atlántida*" (the vestiges of Atlantis), meaning,
of course, the Azores Islands. There are traditions about Atlantis in
the Azores, but these were no doubt brought by the Portuguese,
who found the Azores uninhabited. The inhabitants of the Canary
Islands, as noted by the early Spanish explorers, were a primitive
white race, who had a *written* language, and definite traditions

establishing themselves as the survivors of a former larger island empire. Their survival ended with their rediscovery as they were killed off in a series of wars with the Spanish invaders. We are therefore missing what may have been a fascinating and perhaps the *only* direct link between Atlantis and the present time.

Celtic peoples of western France, Ireland and Wales have memories of ancient contacts with the people from the lands in the sea. In Brittany there are ancient "avenues" of menhirs, colossal upright stones, that go down to the shore of the Atlantic and then *continue* on beneath the sea. While not even the most enthusiastic Atlantologist has suggested that these underwater "roads" lead to Atlantis, they probably *did* lead to Gaulish settlements near the coastline, now submerged, as the French coastline has receded considerably since the land was settled. In a more spiritual sense, however, we may rightly consider that these roads do lead to Atlantis, in that they point like a path leading to a remembered place, drawing one's thoughts to the lost lands under the sea.

If Atlantis did exist and if Atlantis with its civilization was destroyed, why were there not more definite searches organized to find out what had happened? Perhaps to the people living at that time it seemed as if the world had ended and venturing out into the Atlantic under any circumstances was something to be avoided.

As far as we can tell at the present time, the Phoenicians, who some Atlantologists consider to be the survivors of Atlantis, and their descendants, the Carthaginians, were the only people among the ancient navigators to sail past Gibraltar out into the Atlantic. These seafarers went to great pains to keep their profitable trade routes secret, and to discourage the Romans and other competitors from "cutting in" on their trade. They were most willing to perpetuate Plato's reference to "why the sea in those parts is impassable and impenetrable; because there is such a quantity of shallow mud in the way . . . caused by the subsidence of the island. . . ."

The Carthaginian Admiral Himilco is reported by the poet Avienus to have described a voyage on the Atlantic in 500 B.C.: ". . . No breeze drives the ship, so dead is the sluggish wind of this idle sea . . . there is much seaweed among the waves, it holds back the ship like bushes . . . the sea has no great depth, the surface of the earth is barely covered by a little water . . . the monsters of the sea move continuously to and fro and fierce monsters swim among the sluggish and slowly creeping ships. . . ."

Another record from antiquity concerning the Atlantic comes from Pausanias in his *Description of Greece* where he quotes Euphemos the Carian (Phoenician). Euphemos' report, as can be seen, while discouraging any Atlantic voyages, especially discouraged Atlantic travel by women:

> On a voyage to Italy he was driven out of his course by winds and was carried into the outer sea, beyond the course of seamen. He affirmed that there were many uninhabited islands, while in others lived wild men. . . . The islands were called Satyrides by the sailors, and the inhabitants were red-haired, and had upon their flanks tails not much smaller than those of horses. As soon as they caught sight of their visitors, they ran down to the ship without uttering a cry and assaulted the women in the ship. At last the sailors in fear cast a foreign woman on to the island. Her the Satyrs outraged not only in the usual way, but also in a most shocking manner. . . .

Another striking incident did much to discourage Greek investigators of the Ocean. Alexander the Great, after conquering Tyre in

Phoenecia, sent a fleet out to the true ocean for a possible conquest of further Phoenician cities or settlements that might be found beyond the Mediterranean. The fleet sailed out into the ocean—and was heard of no more.

The Carthaginians did their utmost to keep their trade routes in the Atlantic a secret from the Greeks and Egyptians and especially from the Romans. When legends of monsters failed to discourage competition they would often resort to more decisive measures. We find incidents in recorded history where Carthaginian ships, followed past Gibraltar by Roman ships into the open sea, deliberately scuttled themselves rather than divulge their destination. At other times the Carthaginians solved the problem of keeping their trade routes secret by attacking the nearby ship and sinking it with all hands.

Among the lands visited by the Carthaginians in the Atlantic, as reported by Aristotle, was the island of Antilia, a name similar to that of Atlantis. The Carthaginians were so anxious to keep this a secret that the very mention of its name was forbidden under pain of death. It is believed that the Carthaginians conquered Tartessos, a rich and civilized city on the west coast of Spain, near the mouth of the Guadalquivir River, and perhaps the Tarshish mentioned in the bible by Ezekiel who said: "Tarshish was thy merchant by reason of the multitude of all kinds of riches; with silver, iron, tin and lead they traded in thy fairs." In any event Tartessos and its culture disappeared in the sixth century B.C. If Tartessos was, as has been suggested, a colony of Atlantis, this destruction of Tartessos, which was reported to have written records going back 6000 years prior to its disappearance, represents still another possible lost link with Atlantis and its memories.

Myths of lost lands and islands held by the peoples bordering on the eastern Atlantic refer to places the names of which are sometimes reminiscent of Atlantis, as in the case of Avalon, Lyonnesse, Antilla, and sometimes quite different, such as St. Brendan's Island and Brazil, or are simply described, as "the green island under the waves."

The existence of St. Brendan's Island was considered so certain by the Irish that half a dozen expeditions searched for it during the Middle Ages and arrangements were set down in writing for the division of the island when it should finally be found.

Antilla, the same name if not the same island that the Carthaginians were so anxious to keep secret, was thought by the Hispanic peoples to have been a place of refuge from the Moorish conquest of Spain. Refugees escaping the Moors were supposed to have sailed westward, led by a bishop, and to have safely reached Antilla where they built seven cities. Its position on ancient maps is generally given as in the center of the Atlantic Ocean.

The Phoenician and Carthaginian efforts to close the Atlantic to other seafaring nations had the result of perpetuating the idea that the Atlantic was a sea of doom. But mankind never forgot the Fortunate Isles and the other lost lands. They appear again and again on world maps prior to Columbus, sometimes near Spain or on the western rim of the world—Atlantis, Antillia, the Hesperides and the "other islands"; as Plato said, "and from the islands you might pass through the whole of the opposite continent which surrounds the true ocean."

While mankind remembers Atlantis through legends, some animals, birds and marine creatures seem to have conserved an instinctive memory of it as well. The lemming, a Norwegian rodent, follows a curious behavior pattern. Whenever the lemming population explosion causes a food supply problem the lemmings gather in hordes and swarm across the country, crossing rivers along the way, until they get to the sea. Then the great horde enters the water, swimming westwards, until they all drown. Local legends confirm what Atlantologists would naturally suggest—the swarming lemmings are trying to swim to a land that used to be in the west, where food could be found when the local supply gave out.

An even more remarkable behavior pattern, perhaps motivated by memory instinct, has been observed in the behavior of flocks of migratory birds that annually cross the ocean from Europe to South America. As the birds approach the Azores, they begin to fly in great concentric circles, as if searching for land where they might rest. When they don't find it they continue on their way; later they repeat this circling on their return trip. Whether the birds are looking for land or food or both has not been established. The most interesting point of these reports is that man ascribes to the birds the conviction he himself holds, certainly a pleasing and imaginative concept worthy of the days of legend, when man and the animals exchanged their thoughts through speech.

Another animal memory, though not conclusive proof, is even more striking. It concerns the life process of European eels. Strangely enough, Aristotle, sceptical of Plato's account of Atlantis, is involved in this matter which is often cited as proof of Atlantis having existed.

Aristotle, who was interested in all natural phenomena, was the first naturalist on record to bring up the question of multiplication of eels. Where do they breed? Apparently somewhere at sea, for the European eels, every two years, leave their ponds, streams and rivers and swim down the large rivers that empty into the sea. This was all that was known about where eels procreated since Aristotle first asked the question more than 2000 years ago. Only within the last twenty years has the location of the eel breeding grounds been established. The place they have been going to all these centuries is the Sargasso Sea—a weed-filled body of water in the North Atlantic Basin surrounding Bermuda equivalent in size to about half the United States.

The eels' crossing of the Atlantic in a great migratory shoal has been followed because of the flights of gulls overhead and sharks swimming with the shoal and feeding from it as the migration progressed. The shoal takes more than four months to cross the Atlantic. After spawning in the Sargasso Sea at the depth of more than 500 meters, the female eels die and the young eels start the trip back to Europe, where they live for two years before the process is repeated.

It has been suggested that this migration of the eels may be explained by a spawning instinct that leads them back to their ancestral home, perhaps the mouth of a great river which flowed through Atlantis, much as the Mississippi flows through the United States, until it reached the sea.

This spawning instinct of the eels could be compared in difficulty of fulfillment to that of the Alaskan salmon which must fight its way upstream, circumventing dams, while the eel must follow the bed of a river which has vanished, which once flowed through a continent that sunk thousands of years ago.

The Sargasso Sea itself has been variously described as the site of Atlantis or the western sea of Atlantis. A consideration of the sea bottom would indicate that either might be true, as part of the Sargasso covers the tremendous depths of the Hattaras and Nares abyssal plains while another part of it covers the Bermuda Rise with its islands and sea mounts.

The Phoenicians and Carthaginians reported seaweed in parts

of the Atlantic so thick that it impeded the oars of the galleys and held back the ships. If they were referring to the present Sargasso Sea they must have sailed far indeed. However, as the seaweed in the Sargasso is not thick enough to hold back a ship, the Phoenicians were probably using this story as another means of discouraging competition.

Whether the seaweed of the Sargasso Sea is a remnant of sunken Atlantean greenery or not, the Sargasso Sea itself and especially its location is a fascinating subject for speculation.

# 5 ⚓ Into the Ocean's Abyss

To ascertain whether or not Atlantis ever existed, why not examine, as far as we are able, the sea bottom near the location where Atlantis is supposed to have sunk?

Donnelly, who did much to revive popular interest in Atlantis from the 1880's to the present, made a report on the sea bottom soundings of his day in the light of his own study of the Atlantis question. He expressed his feelings on the subject with considerable force and with a conviction which brooked no doubt.

> Suppose we were to find in mid-Atlantic [he wrote] in front of the Mediterranean, in the neighborhood of the Azores, the remains of an immense island, sunk beneath the sea—one thousand miles in width, and two or three thousand miles long—would it not go far to confirm the statement of Plato that, 'beyond the strait where you place the Pillars of Hercules, there was an island larger than Asia (minor) and Libya combined,' called

Atlantis? And suppose we found that the Azores were the mountain peaks of this drowned island, and were torn and rent by tremendous volcanic convulsions; while around them, descending into the sea, were found great strata of lava; and the whole face of the sunken land was covered for thousands of miles with volcanic débris, would we not be obliged to confess that these facts furnished strong corroborative proofs of the truth of Plato's statement, that "in one day and one fatal night there came mighty earthquakes and inundations which engulfed that mighty people? Atlantis disappeared beneath the sea; and then that sea became inaccessible on account of the quantity of mud which the engulfed island left in its place."

And all these things recent investigation has proved conclusively. Deep-sea soundings have been made by ships of different nations; the United States ship Dolphin, the German frigate Gazelle, and the British ships Hydra, Porcupine, and Challenger have mapped out the bottom of the Atlantic, and the result is the revelation of a great elevation, reaching from a point on the coast of the British Islands southwardly to the coast of South America, at Cape Orange, thence south-eastwardly to the coast of Africa, and then southwardly to Tristan d'Acunha. . . . The submerged land . . . rises about 9000 feet from the great Atlantic depths around it, and in the Azores, St. Paul's Rocks, Ascension, and Tristan d'Acunha it reaches the surface of the ocean. . . .

Here then we have the backbone of the ancient continent which once occupied the whole of the Atlantic Ocean, and from whose washings Europe and America were constructed; the deepest parts of the ocean, 3500 fathoms deep, represent those portions which sunk first, to wit, the plains to the east and west

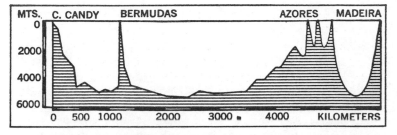

Donnelly's oceanic profile of altitude of the ocean floor from Bermuda to the Madeira Islands.

of the central mountain range; some of the loftiest peaks of this range—the Azores, St. Paul's, Ascension, Tristan d'Acunha— are still above the ocean level; while the great body of Atlantis lies a few hundred fathoms beneath the sea. In these "connecting ridges" we see the pathway which once extended between the New World and the Old, and by means of which the plants and animals of one continent travelled to the other; and by the same avenues black men found their way, as we will show hereafter, from Africa to America, and red men from America to Africa.

And, as I have shown, the same great law which gradually depressed the Atlantic continent, and raised the lands east and west of it, is still at work: the coast of Greenland, which may be regarded as the northern extremity of the Atlantic continent, is still sinking so rapidly that ancient buildings on low rock-islands are now submerged, and the Greenlander has learned by experience never to build near the water's edge. (North America of Antiquity) The same subsidence is going on along the shore of South Carolina and Georgia, while the north of Europe and the

Atlantic coast of South America are rising rapidly. Along the latter raised beaches, 1180 miles long and from 100 to 1300 feet high, have been traced.

When these connecting ridges extended from America to Europe and Africa, they shut off the flow of the tropical waters of the ocean to the north: there was then no Gulf Stream; the land locked ocean that laved the shores of Northern Europe was then intensely cold; and the result was the Glacial Period. When the barriers of Atlantis sunk sufficiently to permit the natural expansion of the heated water of the tropics to the north, the ice and snow which covered Europe gradually disappeared; the Gulf Stream flowed around Atlantis, and it still retains the circular motion first imparted to it by the presence of that island.

The officers of the Challenger found the entire ridge of Atlantis covered with volcanic deposits; these are the subsided mud which, as Plato tells us, rendered the sea impassable after the destruction of the island.

It does not follow that, at the time Atlantis was finally engulfed, the ridges connecting it with America and Africa rose above the water-level; these may have gradually subsided into the sea, or have gone down in cataclysms such as are described in the Central American books. The Atlantis of Plato may have been confined to the 'Dolphin Ridge' of our times.

The United States ship Gettysburg has also made some remarkable discoveries in a neighboring field. . . . 'The recently announced discovery by Commander Gorringe, of the United States sloop Gettysburg, of a bank of soundings bearing N. 85° W., and distant 130 miles from Cape St. Vincent, during the last voyage of the vessel across the Atlantic, taken in connection

with previous soundings obtained in the same region of the
North Atlantic, suggests the probable existence of a submarine
ridge or plateau connecting the island of Madeira with the coast
of Portugal, and the probable subaerial connection in prehistoric times of that island with the south-western extremity of
Europe. . . .'

Sir C. Wyville Thomson found that the specimens of the
fauna of the coast of Brazil, brought up in his dredging-machine,
are similar to those of the western coast of Southern Europe.
This is accounted for by the connecting ridges reaching from
Europe to South America.

A member of the Challenger staff, soon after the termination
of the expedition, gave it as his opinion that the great submarine
plateau is the remains of "the lost Atlantis."

Donnelly did not know, when he wrote the above, about some
later developments in this regard; if he had, his conviction would
have been, if possible, even greater.

The sea bottom has, through sonar and submarine investigation, been defined in much greater detail since Donnelly's day, and,
in the process some curious information about the continental
shelf on both sides of the Atlantic has been discovered as well.

The continental shelf is the land near the shore that is still
geologically part of the land continent before it shelves off into the
depths of the sea and then levels out into what is called the Abyssal
Plain. Examination of the depths of the continental shelves revealed that the beds of rivers which flowed into the Atlantic
continued right on out along the shelf, sometimes going through
canyons just as rivers erode through rock on land. This occurs with
French, Spanish, North African and American river flowing into

the North Atlantic and continue on the bottom along submerged river valleys until they reach a depth of 1½ miles. It is especially striking in the case of the Hudson Canyon which extends the Hudson River bed through underwater cliffs for almost 200 miles to the edge of the continental shelf. It would seem to indicate that these river courses, now thousands of feet under the sea, were cut while that part of the continental shelf was dry land, and that either the land had sunk or the water had risen to cause this inundation of the river beds.

A bulletin of the Geological Society of America (1936) commenting on these sunken river canyons suggests that such "world wide lowering and rising of the sea level . . . amounting to more than 8,000 feet, must have occurred since the late tertiary age. . . ." In other words, the Pleiocene Period—the Age of Man.

Another unusual discovery came about as the result of the breaking of a cable when the transatlantic cable was being laid in 1898, about 500 miles to the north of the Azores. While the cable was being searched for, the sea floor in this area was found to be composed of rough peaks, pinnacles and deep valleys more reminiscent of land than of the sea bottom. Grappling irons brought up rock specimens from a depth of 1700 fathoms which proved, upon examination, to be tachylyte—a vitreous basaltic lava which cools *above water* under *atmospheric pressure*.

According to Pierre Termier, a French geologist who made a study of the incident, if the lava had solidified under water it would have been crystalline instead of vitreous. Termier further surmised that the lava had been submerged under water soon after cooling, as evinced by the relative sharpness of the material brought up. Moreover, as lava decomposes in about 15,000 years, the fact that the underwater lava specimens had not yet decomposed as well as the apparent above-water cooling, fit in extremely well with the theory of Atlantis—even to the timing of the reputed catastrophe, as given by Plato.

Termier further states that ". . . the entire region north of the Azores and perhaps the very region of the Azores, of which they may be only the visible ruins, was very recently submerged, probably during the epoch which the geologists call the present." He recommends ". . . detailed dredging to the south and the southwest of these islands."

Still another missing piece to the puzzle is furnished by the presence of beach sand on underwater shelves, sometimes thousands of feet deep, off the Azores. Beach sand is found on beaches and in shallow water, and is formed by the beating of the surf on the coastal beaches and is not normally present at great depths.

What do we know about the Atlantic Ocean bottom now, many years and many inventions since the times of Donnelly and Termier? A great deal more, thanks to sonar, depth estimation by undersea explosion triangulation, and submarine research. The plains, plateaus, rises, canyons, ridges, deep trenches, cones and the somewhat mysterious seamounts have been charted as well as the islands on the surface, although occasionally a new volcanic island will rise from under the sea and then sometimes sink again before any nation can claim it.

We have, for example, a more exact charting of Dolphin's Ridge, generally called the Mid-Atlantic Ridge, a giant elongated ridge in the shape of two S's, one on top of the other, extending from Iceland to the end of South America. This ridge or plateau with underwater mountains bounded on each side by abyssal plains, becomes quite wide at the semicircle sections of the second "S" between Spain, North Africa and Bermuda. It becomes thin opposite the tip of Brazil south of the equator where the Romanche Fracture zone crosses it and widens out again between southern Brazil and Africa. A striking feature of the Mid-Atlantic Ridge is the fact that it follows the general contour of North and South America, as if it were a thin reflection of the American continents on the ocean bottom.

When we examine the depths around the Azores Islands, we find that although the islands themselves rise precipitously from the bottom, the islands are situated on a sort of double plateau. The base plateau is located from about 30° to 50° North latitude and the higher one from approximately 36° to 42° North with a width of about 500 miles. The depth changes from the plain to the base plateau varies from 1000 to 500 fathoms. That is, if the abyssal depth is, for example, 2400 fathoms, the depth of the ridge may be 1800 fathoms, unless an underwater peak of a seamount reaches 400 fathoms or less, or comes up to a surface island, like the Azores. The second plateau indicates an even more striking rise from 1420 to 400 fathoms; from 1850 to 300 fathoms; from 1100 to 630 fathoms. It is interesting to note that some students of the Atlantis theory have thought that the Atlantean continent went down by stages, perhaps in three subsidences. The double-tiered plateau formation under the Azores would seem to lend some authority to this theory.

South of the Azores we find some important seamounts, not many fathoms below the surface, two of which have been named, with a certain flair, "Plato" (depth 205 fathoms) and "Atlantis" (145 fathoms).

The breaking of the Transatlantic Cable which caused such a furor in Atlantean studies at the beginning of the century took place in the vicinity 500 miles north of the Azores east of the Altair

Seamount. More recent investigations of the ridge have contributed new subjects for speculation.

Bottom samplings or "cores" taken from this ridge in 1957 brought up fresh water plants growing in sedimentary materials at a depth of almost two miles, and examination of sands of the Romanche deep have led them to be considered to have been formed by weathering in parts of the ridge that once projected above the surface.

More than a thousand miles to the west of this mountainous plateau, we find the undersea Bermuda Rise, culminating in the Bermuda Islands, located on the top of immense undersea mountains.

Off the Florida Keys, on the American continental shelf, hydrographic surveys made by the U. S. Geodectic Survey have revealed 400-foot indentations along a 500-foot bottom "presumed to have been fresh water lakes in areas which subsided."

Directly east of the Azores plateau we find the Azores-Gibraltar Ridge, (with depths as shallow as forty to eighty fathoms) and, following south and connected to this ridge down the coast of Africa at relatively shallow depths (also approximately at forty to eighty fathoms), another series of peaks and seamounts which include Madeira and the Canary Islands. The Cape Verde Islands, opposite Dakar, stand alone with no connecting ridges.

Many of the hypothetical "land bridges" between the Old and New Worlds are suggested when we consider the information we now have at our disposal concerning the contour of the sea bottom. For example, the European continental shelf connects, through ridges, with Iceland which in turn connects with Greenland through the Greenland-Iceland Rise. In mid-Atlantic the Azores-Gibraltar Ridge connects with the Azores Plateau and one section

The darker
the tone the greater the depth. ☐ White areas represent land above water.

The Atlantic Ocean as it would appear drained of water.

of the Mid-Atlantic Ridge almost reaches Bermuda, while another smaller ridge breaks off towards the Antilles into the deepest part of the Atlantic Ocean—the Puerto Rico Trench.

Other connecting ridges in the South Atlantic might include a bridge from Africa through the Sierra Leone Rise; then the Mid-Atlantic Ridge through the St. Peter and Paul Rocks to Brazil; or the Walvis Ridge from South Africa crossing the Mid-Atlantic Ridge across to Brazil through the Martin Vaz and Trinidad Islands or the Rio Grande Rise or Bromley Plateau.

Land connection between the Old and New Worlds through land bridges or islands since submerged, which could be used as stepping stones (explaining many curious similarities in plant and animal life, such as the presence of pre-historic elephants, camels and horses in America), are predicated on tremendous changes in the Atlantic sea bottom, caused by volcanic disturbances.

A 1969 Duke University research expedition, engaged in a study of the Caribbean sea bottom, has made an important geological discovery with a distinct bearing on lost continents. During the course of dredging, granitic rocks were brought up from 50 sites along the Aves Ridge, an underwater ridge running from Venezuela to the Virgin Islands. These acid igneous rocks are classified as of a "continental" type, found only on continents or where continents have once been. Dr. Bruce Heezen of the Lamont Geological Observatory said in this regard: "Up to now, geologists generally believed that light granitic, or acid igneous rocks are confined to the continents and that the crust of the earth beneath the sea is composed or heavier, dark-colored basaltic rock, . . . Thus, the occurrence of light-colored granitic rocks may support an old theory that a continent formerly existed in the region of the

eastern Caribbean and that these rocks may represent the core of a
subsided, lost continent."

The bed of the Atlantic is one of the most unstable sections of
the earth's surface. It has been shaken by volcanic disturbances
through the centuries and, in fact, it is still shaking. The volcanic
fault runs from Iceland, where one-fifth of the population perished
in an earthquake in 1783, down the whole length of the Atlantic
Ridge. In 1845 in Iceland the eruption of the Hecla Volcano lasted
for seven months.

Iceland is still in a sometimes furious state of volcanic activity.
A new island, 20 miles off the south-west coast of Iceland, called
Surtsey, was formed in a spectacular continuous submarine eruption lasting from November 1963 to June 1966. Solidified lava
formed land and the island, still growing in size, is developing
permanent vegetation. Since its emergence Surtsey has been joined
by still two other islands. Iceland itself, like Plato's description of
Atlantis, possesses hot springs, so heated by subterranean thermal
forces, that they are used for the heating system of Reykjavik,
Iceland's capital city.

We find persistent records of earthquakes in Ireland, and further down, on a line with the Azores, a tremendous earthquake
shook Lisbon in 1775, killing sixty thousand persons in several
minutes and lowering the level of the principal quay and sinking
docks and quays six hundred feet below the surface of the water.

Volcanic activity is constantly occurring in the Azores area,
where there are still five active volcanos. In 1808 a volcano rose in
San Jorge to a height of several thousand feet, and in 1811 a
volcanic island rose up from the sea, creating a large island which
was called Sambrina during its short above-water existence before it
sank again beneath the sea. The islands of Corvo and Flores in the

Azores, which have been mapped since 1351, have constantly changed their shape, with large parts of Corvo having disappeared into the sea.

In other island groups such as the Canaries, whose large central volcano, the Pico de Teyde, erupted in 1909, the incidence of volcanic disturbances is high. A tremendous earthquake in 1692 sank the greater part of Port Royal into the sea, complete with pirates who were using the city as a refuge, market place and center of rebellion. There is a peculiar reminiscent quality about the sinking of a sinful city into the sea within historic times in the same ocean in which, according to legend, Atlantis was sunk "through divine displeasure."

In the Caribbean, within the Atlantic volcanic zone, an even greater earthquake occurred when Mont Pelée on Martinique blew up with such force in 1902 that it reportedly killed every person, except one, in the adjoining city of St. Pierre. (Like the sparing of Noah?)

In 1931 volcanic activity at the Fernando Noronha group resulted in the appearance of two new islands which Great Britain hastened to claim, although this claim was disputed by several nations of nearby South America. Great Britain was spared an agonizing decision in this matter when the islands sunk again, even while their ownership was still being disputed.

In the Salvage Islands, near Madeira, small islands caused by the emergence of peaks of volcanos rising from the sea-bottom to the surface and beyond, came into existence in 1944. From Iceland to the coasts of Brazil, the Atlantic has been an active volcanic zone through the centuries. According to Dr. Maurice Ewing of the Lamont Geographical Observatory, its deepest rifts "form the locus of an oceanic earthquake belt." It therefore seems logical that

even greater volcanic activity could have taken place thousands of
years ago, especially since such activity is still going on in the very
regions where legend has placed the Atlantean continent.

It is generally agreed that the earth has been the scene of
emergences and submergences of land throughout its surface.
There is ample evidence that the Sahara was once a sea and that
the Mediterranean, with its underwater peaks and valleys, was once
land. Stone age tools and mammoth teeth, dredged up from the
shallow bottom of the North Sea, indicate that it once was coastal
land. Fossils of sharks have been found in the Rocky Mountains,
fish fossils in the Alps and oyster fossils in the strata of the Alle-
gheny Mountains. Most geologists agree that an Atlantean continent once existed, but disagree upon whether it existed within the
Age of Man.

Considerable speculation has been concerned with explaining
the Atlantis legend by other earthquakes and resultant tidal waves
such as the flooding of the former Mediterranean Valley by the sea,
the separation of Sicily from Italy, the catastrophe that overwhelmed Thera in the Aegean, and the Cretan earthquakes of
antiquity. It has also been suggested that Atlantis was in the north,
on the shallow continental shelves under the North Sea, or even in
the Sahara and a variety of other places.

K. Bilau, a German scientist and student of Atlantis, who
devoted much time to the study of the sea bottom and underwater
canyons, speaks for the Atlantis-in-the-Atlantic tradition as he ex-
presses, in language more poetic than scientific, his feelings on the
location of the lost continent. "Deep under the ocean's waters
Atlantis is now reposing and only its highest summits are still
visible in the shape of the Azores. Its cold and hot springs, described by the ancient authors, are still flowing there as they flowed

many millennia ago. The mountain-lakes of Atlantis have been transformed now into submerged ones. If we follow exactly Plato's indications and seek the site of Poseidonis among the half-submerged summits of the Azores, we will find it to the south of the island of Dollabarata. There, upon an eminence, in the middle of a large and comparatively straight valley, which was well-protected from the winds, stood the capital, centre of an unknown prehistoric culture: between us and the City of the Golden Gate is a layer of water two miles deep. It is strange that the scientists have sought Atlantis everywhere, but have given the least attention to this spot, which after all, was clearly indicated by Plato."

# 6 🐛 *How Atlantis Changed History*

For a land that may or may not have existed, Atlantis has had a considerable impact on history as well as on literature. When classical culture, after the fall of Constantinople in 1453, started flowing again into the west, Plato's account, as well as other ancient reports of islands in the Atlantic, once again began to intrigue man's imagination. Columbus, an avid reader of travel accounts and correspondent with cartographers, was not the only one to believe the world was round. Its actual circumference had been calculated in Alexandria in ancient times, with an error of only five hundred miles. But students of the Alexandrine school, although they could measure the earth, never, as far as we know, sailed around it to prove that it was round.

Numerous "world" maps existed at the time of Columbus, although their diverse information, and the fact that the navigational lines were drawn by the stars, would seem to indicate that Columbus' greatest feat of bravery was not in facing the monsters of the sea, or falling off the edge of the world, but in being guided by the maps he had at his disposal.

Some of these world maps showed Antillia, Antilla, Antilha or Antiglia, which may have been alternate names for Atlantis, the Fortunate Isles, the Hesperides and other islands. The Toscanelli map, which Columbus is thought to have had with him on his voyage to the New World, shows Antillia. Years before Columbus made his voyage Toscanelli wrote to him suggesting Antillia as a stopping place on his way to the Indies. On Toscanelli's map China and the Indies were shown on the western shore of the Atlantic, with Antillia and other islands furnishing maritime stepping stones in between.

It is fairly certain that Columbus had studied, or had with him, on his voyage, the Becario map of 1435, and subsequent maps of Branco (1436), Pareto (1455), Rosseli (1468), and Bennicasa (1482) and perhaps material or suggestions from the Benheim map (1492), all of which showed Antillia in its various spellings. These maps generally place Antillia out in the Atlantic on a level with Portugal. In this regard its name in its Portuguese spelling, Antilha (*ante ilha*), becomes logical—it means "the island in front of," "before" or "opposite," referring to the large island in the middle of the ocean, that of the "seven cities." Whether this is the real reason for its name, or whether it is another form of "Atlantis," really comes to the same thing—the large island that had been recommended to Columbus, and that was on all the leading maps, was located at the position generally ascribed to Atlantis and, in disregard of Atlantis' reported sinking, was still shaped like Plato's description of it.

It has also been suggested that Columbus was influenced by an unusual passage from a play by the classical Roman writer, Seneca,

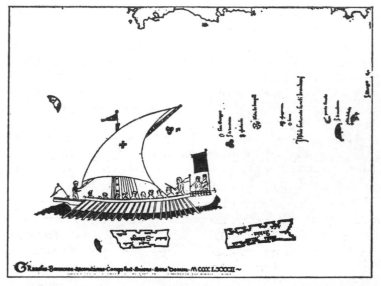

Section of Bennicasa map (1482). The Iberian peninsula is at the top of the map and the ship is pointing due north. To the upper right of the ship are indicated the "Fortunate Isles of St. Brandan," and under the ship, to the left, is a conglomerate called the "Savage Island" and "Antilia."

written centuries before Columbus. The quotation, from *Medea*, Act II, goes as follows: "There will come a time in the late age of the world when the ocean will relax its bonds over what it (now) holds, and land will appear in its glory. Thetis (the sea) will uncover new continents and Thule will no longer be the end of the world. . . ."

Did Seneca get the idea of continents under the ocean from his

imagination, or from Plato or other sources? How generally was
this belief held in classical times? At present we can only guess. But
there is a strong suggestion that Columbus was influenced by this
in his own speculations. One source for this suggestion comes from
one who was personally well acquainted with Columbus and his
ideas—his son, Fernando, who inscribed in a copy of *Medea*—
"This prophecy was fulfilled by my father, the Admiral Christopher Columbus, in 1492."

López de Gomara, author of the *General History of the Indies*
(1552) specifically attributes Columbus' exploits to having "read
Plato's *Timaeus* and *Critias*, where he read of the great Atlantean
island and of a sunken land greater than Asia and Africa."

A claim was actually advanced by Fernández de Oviedo that
the Spanish rulers owned the rights to the New American lands
(*General and Natural History of the Indies*—1525) since, according to him, Hesperus, a prehistoric Spanish king, was the
brother of Atlas, ruler of the opposite land of Morocco, and Hesperus, as part of his domain, also ruled the Hesperides—"The Islands of the West"—"at forty days sail, as they still are, more or less,
in our time. . . . and as Columbus found them to be on the second
voyage he made . . . they therefore must be considered to be these
Indies, lands of Spain since the times of Hesperus . . . which
reverted to Spain (through Columbus). . . ."

A contemporary writer who disagreed was Bartolomé de Las
Casas, a priest who had his own axe to grind. His aim, a very
laudable one, was to protect the Indians of the New World whose
treatment by the Spanish conquerors at this time was assuming
genocidal proportions. De Las Casas took exception to this right of
dominion based on the Hesperides or Atlantis. Nevertheless, in
commenting on Columbus, he observed, in his *History of the*

*Indies*—1527: ". . . Christopher Columbus could reasonably believe and hope that although that great island (Atlantis) was lost and sunken, there would remain others, or at least, dry land, which he could find by searching for it. . . ."

Among other authors at the time of the discovery of the New World, Pedro Sarmiento de Gamboa wrote in 1572: ". . . The Indies of Spain were continents along with the Atlantic Island, and therefore the Atlantic Island itself, which was off Cádiz and extended over the sea which we traverse when we come to the Indies, the sea which all the map makers call the Atlantic Ocean, since the Atlantic Island was in it. And thus we sail now over that which formerly was land."

When the Spanish invaders of Mexico were told that the Aztecs came from a land in the sea called Aztlán they were convinced that the Aztecs were descended from Atlanteans and this reinforced the Spanish right to conquest; not that they ever felt they needed much justification. The very name "Aztec" means people of Az or Aztlán. (The Aztecs usually called themselves Tenocha or Nahua.)

If the Spanish invaders of the New World were influenced, in some respects, by the memory of Atlantis and/or the Hesperides, the Indian population of middle and south America, for another reason, but connected with the same historical or legendary mystique, were so convinced that the Spanish were their civilizing gods or heroes returned from the eastern lands that they became psychologically incapable of resisting them until it was too late.

For many centuries the Toltec, Maya and Aztec nations and other middle American groups, as well as the Chibcha, Aymará and Quechua peoples of South America had preserved legends of mysterious white strangers from the east who had taught them the arts of civilization and subsequently departed, saying they would return.

Quetzalcoatl, the bearded white god of the Aztecs and their predecessors, the Toltecs, was reputed to have sailed back to his own country in the eastern sea—Tollán-Tlapalan—after having founded the Toltec civilization. He said that he would someday return and rule the land again. This same Quetzalcoatl, "the Feathered Serpent," was worshipped among the Mayas as Kukulkán.

When the Spanish arrived in Mexico Moctezuma (Montezuma), the Aztec emperor, as well as many of his subjects, believed that Quetzalcoatl, or at least his messengers, had suddenly reappeared. They even called the Spaniards "teules"—"the gods," especially since their arrival had been announced by numerous portents and prophesies. By a most remarkable coincidence the Spaniards arrived in 1519 at the end of one of the fifty-two year cycles of the Aztec calendar. One of the aspects of this fifty-two year cycle was connected with the recurring birthday of Quetzalcoatl, which made it appear to the bemused Aztecs that Quetzalcoatl, or his messengers were returning on the anniversary of his birth.

Moctezuma's sister, Papantzin, had had a vision of white men coming from the ocean, which was interpreted by Moctezuma and the Aztec priests as a presage of the promised return of Quetzalcoatl. Moctezuma was already half expecting the return of the god when the Spaniards suddenly burst upon him. The emperor instructed his first messengers to greet them with presents "to welcome them home" to Mexico.

The Aztecs were later surprized to see that the homecoming gods ate "human food" and had an ungodlike preference for local

Aztec picture story showing confusion of Moctezuma, the Aztec emperor, as he tries to establish from omens and prophecies whether or not the Conquistadores are messengers of Quetzalcoatl.

maidens in a live, instead of a sacrificed, condition. The Indian population of Mexico who survived the Spanish onslaught were to learn considerably more about "the gods" as they spread their conquests over two continents.

The well organized empire of the Incas in Peru also recorded a prophecy allegedly given by the twelfth Inca. As recounted by Huáscar, his son, to the Spaniards, his father had said that, during the reign of the thirteenth Inca, white men would come from "the Sun, our Father" to rule over Peru. (The thirteenth Inca was Huáscar's brother, Atahualpa, who, as he was being strangled by the Spaniards, perhaps had a moment to fully realize the effective truth of the above prophecy.)

In almost every place they conquered, the Spaniards were helped by legends and beliefs that the Indians themselves held concerning their origins, the origin of their civilization and that the gods would return and rule the land, usually coming from the east. In the study of Atlantis the Amerind (American Indian) legends of an eastern origin is a recurring subject of consideration and often of confusion.

It is generally considered by anthropologists, if not by the Indians themselves, that they came from Siberia, across the Bering Straits and on down through the Americas. General racial characteristics including straight black hair, sparse facial hair, and the "Mongolian spot" on newborn babies, seem to confirm this. Therefore, why these persistent legends about an eastern origin, civilization from the east, and a common legend of a great flood, usually in connection with the destruction or sinking of an eastern homeland?

A possible explanation might be that some Amerinds came from the east or, at least, considerable cultural influences came from that direction. For this reason, perhaps, the tribes would associate themselves with the culture point—a sort of prehistoric version of our own pride in "ancestors-who-came-over-on-the-Mayflower." Cultural indications among Amerinds of Atlantic or Atlantean connections have been noted as including mummification of the dead, common legends, and shared religious practices, similar to those of Europe and the ancient Mediterranean world, such as the use of the cross, baptism, confession, and absolution of sins, fasting and self mortification, and virgins consecrated to religion. These similarities to their own religion caused the Spanish to consider them traps set by the devil. There are also similarities in architecture with Egypt, such as the building of pyramids and other features as well as the hieroglyphic form of writing. Even our existing archeological remains, such as statues and reliefs, not yet accurately dated, show representations of non-Indian peoples, white and black, often dressed in clothing reminiscent of the Mediterranean world. This includes the enormous stone heads found in Tres Zapotes, near Veracruz, which have distinct Negro features, and other smaller statues of the Olmec culture, as well as Mayan representations in statues and on pottery, found at La Venta, of bearded white men, with Semitic noses, wearing clothes, shoes and sometimes helmets, all completely different from those of the Maya. Cylindrical seals and mummy cases with wide bases, like those used in the ancient Mediterranean, found in Palenque, Yucatan, are also peculiar to this part of Mexico, nearest the Atlantic and the North Equatorial current, which flows to the west.

One should also observe that the inhabitants of the New World have been here for a long time; the date of man's appearance in the Americas is constantly being pushed backwards, and now stands at from 12,000 to 30,000 years ago. Besides, all American Indian characteristics are not Northern Asiatic—certainly not the prominent aquiline nose. Frequent reports from early Spanish conquerors and explorers tell of white and black Indians and of many shades between as well as other Amerinds with auburn hair. Some examples of these latter have been found in examination of Peruvian mummies.

It is an oversimplification to declare that all Amerinds and their culture comes from Asia. One student of the subject has left us a thought-provoking commentary on this presumably one-way traffic when he notes that the Indian tribes in their apparent migration from Asia, did not bring any common Asiatic domestic animals with them, as there were none of these in America when the Spaniards first arrived (except a dog, ancestor of the purely Mexican Chihuahua). Considering the presence of the animals that were in America when it was first discovered, he poses the question as to whether the migrating Indians could have dragged or transported wolves, panthers, leopards, deer, crocodiles, monkeys and bears with them as they crossed the Bering Straits, or then peninsula. If these animals did not occur spontaneously on the American continent, then they obviously came by themselves over land bridges, now submerged, from Europe or Africa, and, if the animals could do so—why not the Indians?

Atlantis almost influenced history again in the nineteenth century, through the person of Lord Gladstone, a British Prime Minister during the reign of Queen Victoria, who attempted to get a bill through Parliament to furnish funds to search for Atlantis. The bill was defeated by members of the government who apparently did not share Wm. Gladstone's enthusiasm for the project.

In the 20th century, certain Atlantean societies have been formed in Europe (see Chapter 9), but have not yet assumed a "historical" stature. One of them, the *Principality of Atlantis*, organized by a group of Danish scientists, which subsequently attained a membership of many thousands, chose Prince Christian of Denmark as their leader, with the title of "Prince of Atlantis." (As Prince Christian was a direct descendent of Leif Ericson, the seafaring Viking, and early discoverer of ocean lands, the choice seemed to be a good one.)

While the subject of Atlantis seems far from dead, its future influence on history (except for possible conflict between nations over "risen" Atlantean lands, if they should ever rise, as Cayce foretold), will perhaps take the form of a reassessment of our history and origins. Human pre-history is being pushed farther and farther back through the mists of time. From the Biblical interpretation given by Bishop James Ussher of Dublin in the 17th century that the world started in 4004 B.C., we have progressed to the point that it is now believed that tool-using man alone has been present on earth for several million years, and city culture of the Fertile Crescent goes back at least 9000 years. Archaeology is also in the process of reassessing the first appearance of "civilized" man, whose emergence now appears much earlier than hitherto supposed. There are still many blank spaces in human history and Atlantis may yet prove to be one of them.

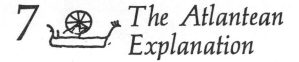
As a cultural, zoological, botanical and anthropological "missing link" between the Old World and the New, Atlantis (or Atlantean land bridges) furnishes a facile explanation of so many things that one might say, paraphrasing Voltaire, if Atlantis had not existed, it would be necessary to invent it.

Culturally Atlantis furnishes an explanation of certain knowledge held in ancient times that could be more easily explained if we supposed the existence of an older civilization, which originally developed knowledge and culture that it passed on to sometimes less productive heirs. For human progress and civilization, as we can see in the Dark Ages and other more modern examples, does not always go progressively forward. Sometimes it seems to hesitate, to stagnate, and even to retreat.

Specific bits of information indicate that the ancient world possessed more scientific knowledge than we would suppose. Besides the geographical knowledge evinced by classical writers in their references to other continents, hints of astronomical knowledge, sometimes confused or disguised in the form of legends, indicated points of ancient knowledge and "know how" subsequently lost with succeeding cultures until rediscovered by the modern world.

For example, how could the ancients have known, without telescopes, that the planet Uranus regularly covered its moons in its course around the sun? This was portrayed by them as the god Uranus alternately eating and disgorging his children. No telescope strong enough to record this phenomenon was in use until relatively modern times.

From what source did Dante Alighieri get his "preview" of the Southern Cross, 200 years before any European had seen or known about it? In the *Divine Comedy* Dante describes what he saw after leaving Hell at the Mountain of Purgatory. The following is a free translation: ". . . I turned to the right, looking toward the other Pole, and I saw four stars, never before seen except by the first people. The sky seemed to sparkle with their rays. Oh, widowed northern region, not being able to see them. . . ." In addition to the mystery of the Southern Cross, to what "first people" was Dante referring?

Every so often an artifact turns up from some ancient culture that is so out of place in time as to be almost incredible. In 1853 a crystalline lens, similar to a modern optical lens, was exhibited at the British Association for the Advancement of Science. It was unique in that it was excavated on the site of Nineveh, the capital of ancient Assyria, representing a time 1900 years before the advent of modern lens grinding.

At Esmeralda, off the coast of Ecuador, pre-Columbia remains brought up from the ocean bottom, and considered by local archaeologists to be of great antiquity, include a convex obsidian lens about 2 inches in diameter, which functions as a mirror, and which reduces but does not distort the reflection. Other very small concave mirrors of hematite, a magnetic iron ore that takes a high polish, have been found in the La Venta excavations of the Olmec civilization of Mexico, now thought to be the most ancient of all the Mexican cultures. Examination shows that these mirrors were ground by an unknown process which made them more curved as the material came closer to the edge. Although their use is not certain experiments have shown that they can be used with the sun to start fires. Other artifacts which appear to be lenses have been unearthed in tombs in Libya, North Africa. And Archimedes, the inventor-scientist of ancient Sicily, used, accordng to Plutarch, optical instruments "to manifest to the eye the largeness of the sun."

Sometimes archaeological finds are not recognized for what they are. The case of the Greek maritime computer of Antikythera is a good example. This was found on an ancient wreck on the bottom of the Aegean in 1900, along with a remarkable collection of statuary, including the famous bronze statue of Poseidon, now in the Athens Museum along with the computer. The purpose of the computer was not originally understood. It seemed to be a combination of bronze plaques, with indistinct writing, fused together by the action of the sea. After cleaning this object and further study it was found to be a computer, with a system of interlocking gears, which apparently served as a sort of slide rule to "shoot" the sun, moon and stars for navigational purposes. This one find has caused considerable change in our attitude towards ancient navigation.

Then there is the case of the Piri Reis map, a world map owned by a Turkish sea captain of the 16th century, which showed the coasts of South America, Africa and portions of Antarctica, although how Antarctica could be included is a mystery. What is even more mysterious is that modern surveys in the Antarctic confirm the accuracy of this map.

The Piri Reis (Reis or Rais being a title of Captain or Master of a vessel) map was reputed to have been compiled from ancient Greek maps which were lost in the destruction of the library at Alexandria. If this map was copied from a variety of ancient maps, it would indicate that important geographic knowledge, available to the ancient world, was lost or forgotten in the Dark Ages.

Some intriguing indications have come down to us from the past concerning the use of other "inventions" hitherto not attributed to ancient times. The use of explosives is a good example as the discovery of gun powder and Greek fire seems to lose itself in the mists of time. The Chinese used explosives as a matter of course before gunpowder was known in Europe. Edgerton Sykes, the leading British authority on Atlantis quotes R. Dikshitar of the University of Madras as claiming the use of explosives to have been known in India as early as 5,000 B.C. The Greek Fire of Byzantium, which helped the Byzantines conserve their empire for a thousand years after the fall of the western Roman Empire, was a mystery then as it is now. It was apparently thrown within shells or with fuses from galleys and, on striking other galleys, would continue to burn despite water thrown on it and would even burn on water.

Explosives may have been used in Europe by Hannibal on several occasions against the Romans. If so, he did not publicize the fact, as it would be psychologically more important for the Romans to think he had superhuman powers at his disposal. The Romans reported the destruction of rocks on his path by fire and subsequent treatment with vinegar and water. Later, at the battle cf Trasymene the earth shook and great rocks crashed down on the Romans who were subsequently defeated by the Carthaginians. It is to be noted that if this were an earthquake it seemed to spare the Carthaginians who immediately profited by it.

In India some years earlier, the troops of Alexander the Great experienced the unnerving incident of having the defenders of an Indian city hurl "thunder and lightening" at them from the walls of a city which they were attacking.

It has even been suggested that the fall of the walls of Jericho was more occasioned by land mines placed in tunnels under them by the attacking Hebrews rather than by the blasts of their trumpets.

In all events, these and other references to something suspiciously like explosives appear again and again in ancient records. Such secret weapons usually appear to have been used by older cultures who inherited them from somewhere else, but the actual race that first employed them is not known.

When one considers the Great Pyramid of Gizeh, it almost seems as if some superior race of craftsman from the past had left a document for future ages, either for their instruction or as a proof of their own scientific knowledge.

Nothing extraordinary, except for its size, had been noted about the Great Pyramid, until Napoleon's surveyors, during the French occupation of Egypt, began to map the country. Naturally enough they chose the Great Pyramid as the starting point of their triangulation and, in dealing with this base, noted first that, if they continued the diagonal lines of the square of the base, they would exactly enclose the Delta of the Nile; and that the meridian passed exactly through the apex of the pyramid, cutting the delta into two equal sections. It was obvious that somebody had planned the pyramid to be at that very place for a special reason. Further study of the measurements of the pyramid indicate that if the perimeter of the base is divided by double its height the figure 3.1416, or pi, is obtained. Its orientation is exact to within 4 minutes 35 seconds. The pyramid is centered on the 30th parallel, which in itself is unusual, as its separates the greater portion of the land surface of the planet from the greater part of ocean surface. From the side of the pyramid that faces due north a gallery extends back to the king's chamber. From the end of this gallery, through millions of tons of perfectly set rock, there is a direct line of sight to the Polar Star which, at the time the pyramid was constructed, belonged to the constellation of the dragon. The height of the Great Pyramid multiplied by a billion gives the distance from the earth to the sun. Each side of the pyramid is found to be equal in cubits to the number of days in the year. Other calculations indicate the weight of the earth and its polar radius and the study of a red granite oblong container found in the king's chamber suggests a whole system of measuring volume and dimension.

Studies of the Great Pyramid have been the subject of many books and are now somewhat in disrepute because of the over-enthusiasm of some writers who professed to see in the measurements of the pyramid and of its inner galleries prophecies concerning the future. This greatest of Egypt's pyramids is apparently the only one that contains, or has been found to contain, such "measurements of record," and there is no indication that Egyptians through the centuries thought there was anything in the pyramid except treasure, or that there was any reason for the pyramid except as the Pharoah's tomb.

There is an element of mystery about the origin of Egypt's civilization in that, about the time of the first dynasty, about 3200

B.C., Egypt changed suddenly from a neolithic culture to an advanced one—almost "overnight" in a historical sense—with effective copper tools, with which they built great palaces and temples and developed an advanced civilization and a sophisticated written language, apparently without having gone through a transitional stage. Where did the Egyptians get their advanced civilization? Manetho, an Egyptian historian at the time of the Ptolomies, said —from the gods, who ruled Egypt before the reign of the first Pharoah, Menes.

The Upanishads, the religious books of India of great antiquity, contain passages that seemed for centuries to be obscure and difficult to interpret. Considered from the point of view of the molecular composition of matter, however, they become fairly easy to understand—another case of scientific knowledge preserved through religious books. We owe our knowledge of zero, or rather, our *use* of zero, to ancient India, from which it came to us via the Arabs, who wrote it as a dot.

But the Maya of Mexico and Guatemala knew about zero as well and used it in chronological and astronomical calculation with amazing accuracy.

An interesting astronomical coincidence existed in the calendar recording of ancient Egypt and Mexico, wherein both calculated, or received the information from another source, that the year is composed of 365 days and 6 hours, based on a division of the months which left 5 complimentary fill-in days at the end of each year, and additional intercalation every cycle, which in the case of the Aztecs was 52 years, and in the case of the Egyptians, 1460 years. Our equivalent date for the beginning of the Aztec year and the Egyptian fixing of their own new year in the month of Thoth was the 26th of February in each case.

But alongside this remarkable mathematical and other scientific knowledge, we find that the Maya and other Amerinds did not recognize the transportation possibilities of the wheel. It used to be thought that none of the Amerinds knew about the wheel at all, until ancient Mexican wheeled *toys* were found in Mexican sites. Perhaps the wheel was once known, then forgotten. It was almost as if the culture were going backward. The Mayan civilization was in a period of decay when the Spanish conquerors arrived, and the great Toltec civilization of Mexico had also vanished, as had the original South American builders of Cuzco and Tihuanaco.

The unusual similarity between Egyptian and Mayan architecture has been evident since the Mayan ruins were first discovered. These include pyramids, columns, obelisks and stelae (but not the true arch), the use of hieroglyphics as architectural ornamentation, bas-reliefs, and stone friezes depicting historical incidents. While other Amerind architecture resembles Egypt's as well, with pyramids and massive constructions, in Central and South America, it is the Mayan architecture, representative of the Indian culture that extends farthest out into the sea which more closely resembles Egypt's.

In considering the origin of Mayan, Olmec and Toltec cultures and that of other pre-Columbian peoples of Central America, we notice that Sahagún, a chronicler of the Spanish conquest, records a curious report gathered from ancient sources that their culture was originally transported to Mexico and Central America from another place. He quotes Indian records: "(They) came from across the water and landed near (Vera Cruz)—the wise old men who had all the writings—the books—the paintings." In this connection Edgarton Sykes, in his annotated edition of Donnelly, offers an interesting explanation of the Mayan custom of abandoning cities and building new ones. If the Mayas came from lands to the east of Central America they must have lived in these land areas that have since submerged, and would have been obliged to abandon their cities, as they sank, and build new ones, which eventually sank as well. This habit of fleeing the sunken lands may explain, Sykes suggests, the tendency of the Maya to abandon one city for another *before* the sea caught up with them. Of course, there remains the generally accepted theory that the Maya left their cities after exhausting the surrounding farm land cleared from the jungle. But there are Mayan ruins off the Mexican coast, under the waters of the Caribbean, as well as the numerous "new" ruins that have recently been discovered from the air, and which are thought by some authorities to be of Mayan or of an even older origin.

The apparent cultural regression or rather lack of forward progress from an advanced starting point, is again evident in the Incan Empire, for the people who preceded the Incas in South America left constructions that defy explanation. When we examine the architectural remains of Peru and Bolivia we find no answer to the question of how they were constructed. The stone blocks of Cuzco fall into two categories—those put in place by the Incas for their palaces and temples, and other basic constructions with fine-cut, exactly fitted stones of enormous proportions, put in place by predecessors of the Incas, of whom only legends remain. How was it possible for primitive people to cut and transport these cyclopean blocks, greater than those of the Egyptian pyramids, over mountainous territory and how, if they possessed only primitive techniques, were the predecessors of the Incas able to fit the blocks together so exactly? And, if they were able to shape the blocks of stone, as they obviously were, why did they not cut them smoothly, which would have been infinitely easier, rather than cut and shape them at odd angles, and then fit them together like a giant jig-saw puzzle? A possible answer to the latter question would be to make the buildings more earthquake-proof, as tremendous land changes through the Andean region have taken place within comparatively recent times.

Another inexplicable cyclopean ruin, that of the city of Tihuanaco, on the shores of Lake Titicaca, in Bolivia, was found abandoned by the first Spaniards who arrived there. It was a city built of enormous stone blocks, some of them weighing up to 200 tons, fastened together by silver bolts. (These silver bolts were taken by the Spanish conquerors, causing the buildings to collapse during subsequent earthquakes). Stone blocks weighing 100 tons had been sunk into the earth as foundations for the supporting walls of these buildings, and door frames ten feet high and two feet thick had been carved from single blocks of stone. According to local legends, the city had been built by the gods. One might believe that the builders were superhuman, because the enormous ruins were located at an altitude of 13,000 feet and located in an arid area now incapable of supporting the large population necessary to build such massive buildings.

Some South American archaeologists consider that Tihuanaco (no one knows what its builders called the city, as there are no records available) was built at a time when the land was almost 2 miles lower than it now is. In fact, an ancient and deserted seaport is located nearby. This theory is based on changes in the Andean Ridge, as interpreted by deposits of calcereous lime or "water mark" lines on cliffs and mountains; and on the assumption that that section of the Andes and Lake Titicaca were thrust upward, destroying and emptying the city, as well as other centers of this prehistoric culture. Remains of mastodons, toxodons and giant sloths found in strata nearby indicate this change of altitude. They could not have lived at the present height, anymore than could the population necessary for building such a city have supported itself in such a high and arid zone. Pictures of these animals have been found on ceramics among the ruins, drawn by the vanished inhabitants of the region.

Local archaeologists have placed the time that Tihuanaco was abandoned as about 10,000 to 12,000 years ago, but much more work in dating has still to be done. However, it must be said that this date, roughly coinciding with that given by the Egyptian priests to Plato for the submergence of Atlantis, is a very convenient one. One part of the world sinks, and another rises, like a great folding or balancing of the earth's surface. In this assumed "folding" there is an intriguing indication that the west coast of South America was affected as well. In the course of a 1966 Duke Oceanographic Program deep-sea cameras photographed carved rock columns on an underwater plain off the coast of Peru, 6,000 feet down, and some depth recorders detected other unusual variations on an otherwise flat bottom.

Dr. Maurice Ewing of the Lamont Geological Observatory has stated in regard to the rift system and oceanic earthquake belts: ". . . The opposite effect of tension is compression, which results in a folding of the earth's surface. The mountain systems of the continents, such as the Rockies and the Andes, were probably caused by such a folding."

Other hints of prehistoric civilization in South America are somewhat baffling, like the wheeled toys of ancient Mexico. There is a tradition that the ancient Peruvians had developed a system of hieroglyphic writing, along the lines of that developed by the

Central American Civilizations, but that the Incas prohibited it (as non-productive?) and instituted their own memory system of knotted and colored cords. These cords, used to record tribute, taxes and census, may have been in themselves a form of writing, or a sort of ancient computer response system.

Then there are some constructions so huge that they are hard to believe. A huge hill at Cholula, Mexico, was originally a pyramid, now crowned by a church. It is reputed to have been built as a refuge from future floods, but a confusion of languages scattered the builders (a legend with a somewhat familiar ring)! A mountain outside Quito, Ecuador, has such a regular shape that some observ-

Comparison of false or corbelled arch in ruins at Palenque, Mexico, and Mycenae, Greece.

ers consider it to be artificial, in other words a giant pyramid, but the general impression is that it is simply too big to be man-made. The huge Toltec and Aztec pyramids were *bases* for temples at the top—causing the Spaniards to marvel at these "mansions in the sky."

We find analogous massive monuments and cyclopean stonework throughout the Atlantic world and the early Mediterranean. The mysterious monolithic circles of Stonehenge, the dolmens of Brittany and Cornwall, the neolithic forts in Ireland, Aran and the Canary Islands, cyclopean walls in Southern Spain, the continuation of the "pyramid belt" from America through Etruria and North Africa to Mesopotamia, stone palaces, tombs, temples or cave complexes in Sardinia, Malta the Balearic Islands, and in archaic Greece and Mycenae similar cyclopean architecture as well as the same corbelled arch used in Yucatan.

Some of these megalithic structures may have had purposes known to the builders but not immediately apparent to us. Huge stone circles at Stonehenge, England, which are not only of interest because of the size of the stones and the question of how they were transported and set in place, but even more so for the reasoned pattern for their erection. The central axis of Stonehenge was constructed to correlate exactly with sunrise in midsummer. Other findings appear to confirm the purpose of Stonehenge as an enormous astronomical clock and its exact correlations reflect knowledge on the part of its builders not only of astronomy but of trigonometry as well.

Another series of stone calendar constructions and huge flat designs drawn on the ground but completely visible only from *above* is located nearby at Avebury. These are so huge in scope that their stone pattern could only be realized and appreciated through aerial photography. Cornwall, where many mysterious dolmens are located, is a peninsula, the part of England pointing out furthest into the Atlantic, perhaps towards the place from where the original builders came, to construct what appears to be huge "planetary clocks" of stone.

Across the Atlantic, in the desert region about 160 miles south of Lima, Peru, is an amazing series of geometric patterns together with huge ground-drawn pictures of birds, animals and people covering a 200 square mile area. The pictures traced on the earth are so large that they can only be seen from the air and one wonders how the artists could have been sure of what they were doing without some means of checking or observing from above.

Even more unusual are the intricate series of trapezoidal lines and strips which, like the pictures, were not recognized until they were noticed, in 1939, from a plane which was being used by a history professor studying ancient irrigation techniques.

These drawings are thought to have been made by the pre-Inca Nazca Indian people who have since disappeared. One theory is that they were connected with the relationship of stars to the solstice and equinox lines during the Nazca era, in other words, an enormous astronomical calendar reminiscent of Stonehenge and Avebury. Local legend attributes them to the goddess Orichana who descended to earth in "a ship of the sky as brilliant as the sun." (One might suggest that she needed an airship to appreciate the patterns, or that possibly these patterns and strips had something to do with landing facilities).

In any event, descendents or the present day indigenous inhabitants of certain areas where these unusual and what may be "functional" monuments are found have evidently forgotten the purpose for which they were constructed.

In Brittany long lines of menhirs (huge standing stones) and the intricately balanced dolmens (boulders balanced on top of a group of standing boulders) may also be connected with observations of time or season. But one of the dolmens, called "The Talking Rock," has in recent times been used for fortune-telling purposes, apparently indicating by a tilt of its huge bulk a "yes" or "no" answer when questioned.

Then there is the cultural riddle of the very ancient cave paintings in Europe, at Lascaux, Altamira and other sites, as well as cave paintings in the Sahara in Africa, from the time when the Sahara had not yet become a desert. These magic or hunting paintings of animals are located in various caverns of Spain, France and Africa. They are generally considered the work of the "Crô-Magnon" man, a preglacial culture of about 30,000 years ago. Some of these paintings are crude, but others tend to be so sophisticated in style, composition and treatment that it appears that different prehistoric groups used these caverns. Among these were some who possessed a highly developed and stylized art which must have taken centuries to develop. When one examines it, across more than 30,000 years, it looks strangely modern, unlike many art periods of the intervening centuries. From where did this race of developed artists suddenly appear in Western Europe and North Africa? Were they refugees from a sunken area in the Atlantic Ocean?

None of the above similarities or seemingly related architectural forms, however, furnishes any proof of the existence of Atlantis. It is, at present, only an assumption or an "informed guess" which, if true, would cause many seemingly disconnected bits of information to fall into place.

One might call this the "Atlantean Explanation" of pre-history based on the assumed existence of a former Atlantic continent or

Pre-historic cave art from Altamira, Spain, showing sophisticated treatment of painting on rock slightly raised and following the animal in shape.

Aurignacian horse head from cave at Mas d'Azil, France.

land bridge between the Americas and Europe. This predicated land connection would also explain the bones of mammoths or elephants, lions, tigers, camels and primitive horses having been found in America. Although none of these were here when the Spanish arrived, their remains have been positively identified. Bochica, the teacher who brought civilization to the Chicha nation of Colombia, is reported by legends to have arrived in Colombia, with his wife, riding on camels.

The elephant, or perhaps mammoth, is frequently a motif in Amerind art or architecture. Did the pre-Columbian Indians see them or did they reconstruct them from examining their bones? In

Outline of large pre-Columbian "Elephant" mound in Wisconsin (from above), and pipe found inside mound in Iowa.

any event, they seemed to know about elephant's trunks. Elephant head decorations and elephant masks on bas-relief have been found at Palenque, Yucatan and a large mound, in the clear vertical shape of an elephant still exists in Wisconsin. It is called, appropriately enough, Elephant Mound. Other representations of elephants occur on pipes, discovered in another Indian mound in Iowa. In pre-Columbian Central America, golden, winged elephants worn on a chain as neck ornaments, have been found. (In reference to this

latter case, an Italian critic has suggested, in refutation, that elephants don't have wings today and probably didn't then. But what
about winged horses in our own art and legend, such as Pegasus?)

A. Braghine, in his book "The Shadow of Atlantis," suggests
another connection between elephants and mammoths and the
land changes contemporaneous with the supposed sinking of Atlantis. He draws a parellel between the numerous mammoths found
frozen in Siberia judged to be 12,000 years old and a whole field of
mastodon bones found in Colombia, near Bogotá. In each case he
predicates the death of the animals on a sudden climate change.
Some of the Siberian mammoths were found frozen standing up
with undigested food still in their stomachs. But the food they
were eating is no longer to be found in the area. It is further
suggested that these mammoths were drowned in a sea of mud
which subsequently froze. In Colombia the sudden death of the
mastodons, as indicated by the quantity of bones found at one spot
near Bogotá, is ascribed by Braghine to a sudden raising of the
ground on which they were grazing. Both of these phenomena are
calculated to have taken place at the same time—the rising of
South America and the flooding of the Siberian marshes—at the
approximate period in the world's history indicated by Plato for the
sinking of Atlantis.

More humble animals have also been cited to lend further
proof to the theory of land connections. The same kind of earth-
worms are present in Europe, North Africa and the islands of the
Atlantic. A crustacean, the fresh water capod, is common to Europe and America. Species of burrowing beetles are common only
to America, Africa and the Mediterranean. Of the butterflies found
in the Azores and the Canary Islands two-thirds are common to
Europe and about one-fifth to America. A certain mollusk, the olea-

Ancient Mexican representation of an elephant, or a figure wearing an elephant mask.

cinida, is found only in Central America, the Antilles, Portugal *and* the Azores and Canaries. As mollusks are attached to shore rocks and shelves near the shore, and expand their fields only at certain temperatures, some shallow land connections must have existed to account for their presence at such widely separated points.

A black saltwater tidal pond exists in a cave in Lanzarote, near Cueva de los Verdes in the Canary Islands. In this pond there are small crustaceans named *munidopsis polymorpha* which are blind and exist nowhere else. A non-blind related species, the *munidopsis tridentata* lives at that may be the submarine exist of this Atlantic pond, almost half a mile down in the ocean. Scientists who have studied this question believe that the blind munidopsis were trapped in the subterranean pond thousands of years ago, and thereby gradually lost their sight.

Rabbits were found in the Azores Islands when they were discovered, implying a land connection of some sort, unless the

Carthagenians, which seems unlikely, imported them to the Azores.

To return to larger animals, the presence of men, cattle, sheep and dogs on the Canary Islands, when they were discovered in the 14th century would be easier to explain, as these islands are relatively close to Africa, except for one thing—the inhabitants of the Canary Islands, when they were discovered, *had no boats*, certainly an unusual lack for islanders.

Moreover, the monk seal is found off the Azores, although generally seals would not go to the middle of the ocean. The Atlantean hypothesis would explain that the seals probably followed a coastline which almost united the Old and New Worlds, but were biologically marooned, like other animals, by the catastrophe. One is reminded, in this connection, of Aelian's report about the "sea rams" from whose skins the "Rulers of Atlantis" fashioned their headbands.

Were all of the fauna of the Atlantic Islands, mollusks, crustaceans, butterflies, rabbits, goats, seals and people, biological survivors marooned on the same small islands, the mountain peaks of a sunken continent?

Finally, there is the matter of the Bronze Age itself. Man started using bronze, an alloy of copper and tin, many centuries before using iron. Moreover, the use of bronze was common in Western and Northern Europe as well as the Mediterranean, and was known to the Incas of Peru and the Aztecs of Mexico. The bronze age cultures of Spain, France, Italy, North Africa and even Northern Europe are constantly giving evidence of a much higher civilization than was previously supposed.

While, as far as we know, the American Indians never developed bronze, they produced certain amalgams of copper. Copper mines near Lake Superior give indications of prehistoric mining operations as far back as 6000 B.C. Other Indian peoples were skilled metalurgists. Those of Mexico and Central America have left us intricate and beautiful artifacts and jewelry made of precious metals. The Incas of Peru mined enormous quantities of gold and silver, which were not used for money but for articles of beauty, with emphasis on purposes of religion and the imperial household. Gold was called "Tears of the Sun" and silver "Tears of the Moon"; the gardens of the Inca, according to first-hand reports of the Spanish conquerors, contained skillfully wrought silver trees on which perched golden birds.

The use of forged iron apparently came from Central Asia, spreading east and west, while its predecessor, bronze, existed in an area which can be described as a great circle around the Atlantic, from the Americas to Northern Europe and inward to the Mediterranean.

An especially interesting example of the Bronze Age in the Mediterranean is the Etruscan culture whose bronze chariots and bronze weapons were unable to withstand the Romans, and thereupon vanished from history, leaving records written in an alphabet which has not yet been translated. It is a striking coincidence that Plato specifically mentions the country of the Etruscans, Liguria, as being a colony of Atlantis.

The Bronze Age culture extended to North Africa as far as Nigeria, where the ancient Yoruba people developed an advanced and sophisticated civilization. Among other bronze statues found at Ife, Nigeria, an especially interesting example is that of the head of Olokun, God of the Sea, like Poseidon, also Lord of the Sea— and earthquakes!

As one considers the similarities of prehistoric bronze age cultures in terms of an arc around the Eastern Atlantic and its "inlet," the Mediterranean, one might well be reminded of the similarity of names also describing roughly the same arc—Atlas, Antilla, Avalon, Arallu, Ys, Lyonesse, Az, Ad, Atlantic, Atalaya, as well as the "American" names of Aztlán, Atlán, Tlapallan etc.—these names given to a lost land or paradise, the original land or the land from where teachers came—located in the Western or Eastern Sea, depending on which side of the ocean the legends were current.

If we were trying to solve some of the mysteries of prehistory, how many things Atlantis would explain! By the hypothesis of a central point in the Atlantic for the growth and distribution of an important prehistoric civilization which vanished through a catastrophe we could explain baffling cultural coincidences and common flood legends between the Old and New Worlds; the distribution of certain animals and peoples; the rising and sinking of land masses; indications of recesses of civilization; of lost knowledge and techniques preserved only in legends; evidences of sophisiticated art in prehistoric periods; and, in short, the origin and spread of civilization itself. But, however convenient, the hypothesis may be, it is, for lack of more conclusive evidence, still a theory—and theories need proof.

We have progressed in the course of our scientific investigation of the present looking to the future to a position where we are now immeasurably better equipped to reexamine the past. The date of the origin of civilization has been pushed further and further back in time to a point previously covered only by legends—to the past so distant that it is roughly equivalent to the time Plato gave for the sinking of Atlantis. In other words, through modern knowledge, archaeological research, dating techniques, breakdown of undeciphered scripts through use of computers, and facilities for undersea exploration, we are now in a better position than at any time in our history to find out when civilization began, and, at the same time, to prove or disprove the Atlantis theory. For although some theories previously held about Atlantis have been discredited in the light of subsequent examination, still other developments and some discoveries have reaffirmed certain elements in the Atlantis theory and even suggested new ones.

# 8 ⚓ *Some Theories About Atlantis*

Philosophers and writers from the time of the discovery of the Americas to the present have given us their theories about Atlantis. Francis Bacon, for example, in *The New Atlantis*, 1638, expressed the opinion that the Atlantis of Plato was simply America. Shakespeare's plot for *The Tempest*, set as it is on an Atlantic Isle, is sometimes ascribed to the renewed interest in Atlantis and lost islands in the Atlantic. Later, in 1665, Father Kirsher, a Jesuit student of the question, reaffirmed the opinion that Atlantis was an Atlantic island, and has left us a famous map of Atlantis and its relation to Europe and America, although the map itself is, to our way of looking at it, upside down, as the top is south.

Even Voltaire got into the act, or was so credited, through a dedication to Voltaire on the part of Jean Bailly, a French astronomer prior to the French Revolution, in a study of Atlantis, which he placed in the far north, when the Arctic was tropical. Voltaire was thought to have shared the opinion of Bailly, although this is

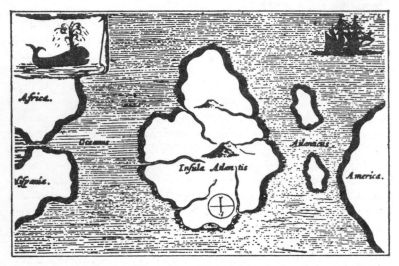

Father Kircher's 17th century map of Atlantis (north is at bottom), with inscription reading: "Site of the Island of Atlantis now swallowed up by the sea, according to the belief of the Egyptians and Plato's description."

difficult to prove, especially in view of Voltaire's lack of faith in most of the institutions of his day.

It is well known that parts of the Arctic and the Antarctic *were* tropical. Bulldozers in Alaska, Northern Canada, and Greenland today have sometimes unearthed saber-toothed tigers and other animals whose habitat suggests a warmer climate. But this, in itself, has no immediate bearing on the subject of Atlantis, other than being another indication of the great climatic changes which the world has undergone.

Among other more modern theories about Atlantis, two important schools appeared in the nineteenth century, one based on Atlantis as an Atlantic island, a bridge between America and Europe, and the other supposing Atlantis to have been located in North or Northwest Africa, at a time when the Sahara was not yet a desert.

The former theory was given an enormous impetus in 1882 by Ignatious Donnelly, whose book *Atlantis—Myths of the Antediluvian World*, which went into fifty editions and is still being republished, has had so much influence upon Atlantean studies that it merits, with all its frequent errors and enthusiastic exaggerations, a close and even a rather sympathetic examination, considering the time when it was written. For sheer brio and assured conviction it has not been equaled since.

Donnelly may have been influenced in his theory about Atlantis by Bory de Saint-Vincent, who, in 1803, wrote an article indicating that the Azores and the Canary Islands were remnants of Atlantis, and who designed a map of Atlantis based on information from classical writers. Donnelly was also probably influenced by Brasseur de Bourbourg and Le Plongeon, two French scholars who lived in Mexico and Guatamala, learned the Mayan language, and subsequently made interpretive and unverified translations of portions of the few surviving Mayan records, by which they attempted to prove that the Mayas were descendants of fugitives from Atlantis. Donnelly may also have been influenced by Hosea, (1875), an American student who equated American Indian cultures with that of Egypt.

Donnelly theorized that Atlantis was the first world civilization, the colonizing and civilizing power of the Atlantic littoral, the shores of the Atlantic, the Mediterranean, the Caucasus, South and Central America, the Mississippi Valley, the Baltic and even India and parts of Central Asia, and the place where the alphabet was invented. He took the catastrophic sinking of Atlantis as a historic fact, immortalized in flood legends, and thought that the myths and legends of antiquity were simply a misty or muddled version of factual Atlantean history.

Donnelly attempted a scientific approach to the subject, examining the plausibility of Plato's story and considering historical earthquakes and sinking of cataclysmic proportions and the rising and disappearance of islands in the sea.

As proof that such a colossal sinking could occur, he examines earthquakes which caused land submergences in the past, in Java and Sumatra, Sicily, and a 2,000 square mile land sinking off the Indus.

But it is the Atlantic Ocean that seems to him to be the most unstable and changeable zone of all. He mentions the eighteenth century earthquakes in Iceland and the appearance of an island claimed by the king of Denmark, but which sunk again. Also in the eighteenth century the Canary Islands "probably a part of the original empire of Atlantis" were shaken by earthquakes that went on for a five year period. In describing the great earthquake of Lisbon, also in the eighteenth century "that point of the European coast nearest to the site of Atlantis," he says: ". . . In six minutes 60,000 persons perished. A great concourse of people had collected for safety upon a new quay, built entirely of marble; but suddenly it sunk down with all the people on it, and not one of the dead bodies ever floated to the surface. A great number of small boats and vessels anchored near it, and, full of people, were swallowed up as in a whirlpool.

No fragments of these wrecks ever rose again to the surface; the water where the quay went down is now 600 feet deep. The area covered by this earthquake was very great. Humboldt says that a portion of *the earth's surface, four times as great as the size of Europe, was simultaneously shaken.* It extended from the Baltic to the West Indies and from Canada to Algiers. At eight leagu from Morocco the ground opened and swallowed a village of ֽ0,000 inhabitants, and closed again over them.

"It is very possible that the center of the convulsion was in the bed of the Atlantic, and that it was a successor of the great earth throe which, thousands of years before, had brought destruction upon that land." Donnelly's description of the Atlantic earthquake belt continues: ". . . While we find Lisbon and Ireland, east of Atlantis, subjected to these great earthquake shocks, the West India Islands, west of the same center, have been repeatedly visited in a similar manner. In 1692 Jamaica suffered from a violent earthquake. . . . A tract of land near the town of Port Royal, about a thousand acres in extent, sank down in less than one minute, and the sea immediately rolled in."

Although Donnelly, writing before 1882, could not foresee the destruction of Martinique occasioned by Mount Pelée in 1901, we can assume that his sadness about the fatalities would have been mitigated by the support the catastrophe lent to his theories.

When Donnelly comes to the Azores, "undoubtedly the peaks of the mountains of Atlantis" he considers that the volcanoes that sunk Atlantis may reserve a surprise for the future: ". . . In 1808 a volcano rose suddenly in San Jorge to the height of 3,500 feet, and burned for six days, desolating the entire island. In 1811 a volcano rose from the sea, near San Miguel, creating an island 300 feet high, which was named Sambrina, but which soon sunk beneath the sea. Similar volcanic eruptions occurred in the Azores in 1691 and 1720:

> Along a great line, a mighty fracture in the surface of the globe, stretching north and south through the Atlantic, we find a continuous series of active or extinct volcanoes. In Iceland we have Oerafa, Hecla, and Rauda Kamba; another in Pico, in the Azores; the peak of Teneriffe; Fogo, in one of the Cape de Verde Islands: while of extinct volcanoes we have several in Iceland, and two in Madeira; while Fernando de Noronha, the island of Ascension, St. Helena, and Tristan d'Acunha are all of volcanic origin. . . .

> These facts would seem to show that the great fires which destroyed Atlantis are still smouldering in the depths of the ocean; that the vast oscillations which carried Plato's continent beneath the sea may again bring it, with all its buried treasures, to the light. . . .

Besides proposing the diffusion of certain animals as a proof of "land bridges" across the Atlantic, Donnelly suggests that the banana and other seedless plants were carried to America by civilized man and quotes Professor Kuntze:

"A cultivated plant which does not possess seeds must have been under culture *for a very long period*—we have not in Europe a single exclusively seedless, berry-bearing, cultivated plant—and hence it is perhaps fair to infer that these plants *were cultivated as early as the beginning of the middle of the Diluvial Period.*"

To this Donnelly adds with categoric certainty: ". . . We find just such a civilization as was necessary, according to Plato, and under just such a climate, in Atlantis and nowhere else. We have found it reaching, by its contiguous islands, within one hundred and fifty miles of the coast of Europe on one side, and almost touching the West India Islands on the other, while, by its connecting ridges, it bound together Brazil and Africa."

Donnelly examined in detail the common world flood legends as further proof of the sinking of Atlantis. He makes a point of a particular detail—the mention of mud after the flood, which, according to Plato (and the Phoenicians) made the Atlantic unnavigable after the disappearance of Atlantis. He says: ". . . This is one of the points of Plato's story which provoked the incredulity and ridicule of the ancient, and even of the modern world. We find in the Chaldean legend something of the same kind: Khasisatra says, 'I looked at the sea attentively, observing, and the whole of humanity had returned to mud.' In the legends of the 'Popol Vuh' we are told that a 'resinous thickness descended from heaven.'

"*The explorations of the ship* Challenger *show that the whole of the submerged ridge of which Atlantis is a part is to this day thickly covered with volcanic debris.*

"*We have but to remember the cities of Pompeii and Herculaneum, which were covered with such a mass of volcanic ashes from the eruptions of 79 A.D. that for seventeen centuries they remained buried at a depth of from fifteen to thirty feet. . . .*

"*. . . In 1783 the volcanic eruption in Iceland covered the sea with pumice for a distance of one hundred and fifty miles, 'and ships were considerably impeded in their course.'*

"*. . . The eruption in the island of Sumbawa, in April 1815, threw out . . . a mass two feet thick and several miles in extent, through which ships with difficulty forced their way.*

"*It thus appears that the very statement of Plato which has* provoked the ridicule of scholars is in itself one of the corroborating features in his story. It is probable that the ships of the Atlanteans, when they returned after the tempest to look for their country, found the sea impassable from the masses of volcanic ashes and pumice. They returned terrified to the shores of Europe; and the shock inflicted by the destruction of Atlantis upon the civilization of the world probably led to one of those retrograde periods in the history of our race in which they lost all intercourse with the Western continent."

In his enthusiasm for the Atlantean explanation of history Donnelly claimed that until fairly modern times ". . . nearly all the arts essential to civilization which we possess date back to the time of Atlantis—certainly to that ancient Egyptian civilization which was coeval with, and an outgrowth from, Atlantis.

*"In six thousand years the world made no advance on the civilization which it received from Atlantis."*

In pointing out the antiquity of the important inventions of early civilization, he suggests that they came from a central point. He states in support of this supposition: ". . . I cannot believe that the great inventions were duplicated spontaneously, as some would have us believe, in different countries; there is no truth in the theory that men pressed by necessity will always hit on the same invention to relieve their wants. If this were so, all savages would have invented the boomerang; all savages would possess pottery, bows and arrows, slings, tents and canoes; in short, all races would have risen to civilization, for certainly the comforts of life are as agreeable to one people as another.

". . . Every civilized race in the world has had something of civilization from the earliest ages; and as 'all roads lead to Rome' so

PHOTO BY JIM THORNE

Photo taken at depth of over 100 feet showing ruins of ancient
city 1000 feet offshore from the island of Melos in the Aegean
Sea, the island of "Venus de Milo." Column on left is broken
but still in place as is wall on right, just as they were when the
city fell into the sea, probably as the result of a volcanic
eruption.

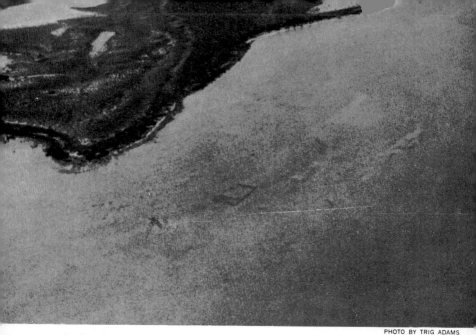

PHOTO BY TRIG ADAMS

Aerial view of underwater "ruin" off Andros Island in the Caribbean. Discovery of this and similar constructions have lent considerable credence to Edgar Cayce's prediction, made in 1924, that Atlantean ruins would emerge from the sea in 1968 or 1969.

Closer view of underwater building which is considered to resemble Maya architecture.

PHOTO BY TRIG ADAMS

PHOTO BY ADELAIDE DE MESNIL

Aerial view of sunken port section of Cenchreai in the Aegean Sea, indicating subsidence of coastal lands in the Mediterranean. The old water line can be seen in the dock area near the boat and the lower right hand corner. Ruins at extreme left are above water.

shops and forges; of sword-making, engraving and metallurgy; of wine, barley, wheat, cattle, sheep, horses and agriculture generally. Who can doubt that it represents the history of a real people? . . ." and concludes: ". . . The entire Greek mythology is the recollection, by a degenerate race, of a vast, mighty, and highly civilized empire, which in a remote past covered large parts of Europe, Asia, Africa, and America. . . ."

He suggests an attractive explanation as to how Atlantean historical figures became gods of other nations when he proposes (and we must remember that he was writing at a time when the British Empire was in the heyday of its power).

". . . Let us suppose that Great Britain should tomorrow meet with a similar fate. What a wild consternation would fall on her colonies and upon the whole human family! . . . . William the Conqueror, Richard Coeur de Lion, Alfred the Great, Cromwell, and Victoria might survive only as the gods or demons of later races; but the memory of the cataclysm in which the center of a universal empire instantaneously went down to death would never be forgotten; it would survive in fragments, more or less complete, in every land on earth. . . ."

A pleasant echo of Donnelly's supposition that the stories of Greek gods were really history was given by Edgar Daqué, a French writer of fifty years later. Among other geographical theories Daqué viewed the legend of the Pleiades—the daughters of Atlas who changed into stars—as an allegory explaining the disappearance of parts of the Atlas mountain range beneath the sea. In other words, parts of the body of Atlas, his daughters, disappeared and became stars—the Pleiades—while their former shapes, when they were mountains, still lie under the Atlantic. He also explains the quest of Hercules to the Hesperides for golden apples as an allegory for Greek trading with a more civilized culture in the Atlantic. The golden apples were, in his opinion, oranges or lemons, and he thought that the western culture (Atlantis) probably had different grains and "better developed types of fruits and produce (which would) arouse the envy of the poorer Mediterranean races. . . ." One is reminded of the theory of the alleged Atlantean development of the banana and the pineapple. (One notes that the Italian word for tomato, unknown in Europe before the discovery of America, is *pomodoro*—"golden apple.")

Donnelly also makes a case for the Phoenician gods being memories of Atlantean rulers, and, in fact, considers the Phoenicians nearer to the Atlanteans than were the Greeks, and the means by which elements of the older culture were passed on to the Greeks, Egyptians, Hebrews and others. ". . . The extent of country covered by the commerce of the Phoenicians represents to some degree the area of the old Atlantean Empire. Their colonies and trading posts extended east and west from the shores of the Black Sea, through the Mediterranean to the west coast of Africa and of Spain, and around to Ireland and England; while from north to south they ranged from the Baltic to the Persian Gulf. . . . Strabo estimated that they had three hundred cities along the west coast of Africa. . . ."

He neatly connects Columbus who, according to one theory held in the Spanish-speaking world, was of Jewish origin, with the Semitic Phoenicians by saying: ". . . When Columbus sailed to discover a new world, or re-discover an old one, he took his departure from a Phoenician seaport, founded by that great race two thousand five hundred years previously. This Atlantean sailor, with his Phoenician features, sailing from an Atlantean port, simply re-opened the path of commerce and colonization which had been closed when Plato's island sunk in the sea. . . ."

Donnelly envisions the Atlantean Empire as a prehistoric empire extending over most of the world. Most of his work involved tracing Atlantean legends, influences and even relics, specifically in Peru, Colombia, Bolivia, Central America, Mexico and the Mississippi Valley, where he connected the Mound Builder Culture with Atlantis; in Ireland, Spain, North Africa, Egypt, and especially Pre-Roman Italy, Great Britain, the Baltic regions, Arabia, Mesopotamia and even India. He waxes eloquent over:

". . . An empire which reached from the Andes to Hindustan . . . in its market must have met the maize of the Mississippi Valley, the copper of Lake Superior, the gold and silver of Peru and Mexico, the spices of India, the tin of Wales and Cornwall, the bronze of Iberia, the amber of the Baltic, the wheat and barley of Greece, Italy and Switzerland. . . ."

His enthusiastic beliefs are almost catching as he refers to the Atlanteans as: ". . . the founders of nearly all our arts and sciences; they were the parents of our fundamental beliefs; they were the first civilizers, the first navigators, the first merchants, the first colonizers of the earth; their civilization was old when Egypt was young, and they had passed away thousands of years before Babylon, Rome or London were dreamed of. This lost people were our ancestors, their blood flows in our veins; the words we use every day were heard, in their primitive form, in their cities, courts and temples. Every line of race and thought, of blood and belief, leads back to them. . . ."

In his desire to prove the theory in which he so enthusiastically believed Donnelly, and many others who have shared this same general theory, often assumed cultural and racial similarities which have since been disproved, especially linguistic connections which were often in error. Perhaps a good example of the lengths to which a preconceived idea can lead researchers is seen in the translation of the Mayan Codex Troano (part of one of the three remaining Maya written records which had escaped the general conflagration initiated by Bishop Landa, who was Bishop of Yucatán in the 16th century) attempted by Brasseur de Bourbourg and later by Le Plongeon, both of the 19th century, in the course of their research on the question of Atlantis and their attempt to link the Mayan civilization of Yucatán to that of Atlantis.

In 1864, Brasseur de Bourbourg discovered in the Madrid archives a Mayan alphabet compiled by Bishop Landa (who was, ironically enough, the man who did more than any other to destroy all Mayan literature). This alphabet was based on a complete misconception because Landa, in trying to approximate the Mayan alphabet, did not realize that the Mayas probably did not have an alphabet, but probably a mixture of hieroglyphics and phonetic symbols. Therefore, by asking the letter for "a," "b," "c," and so forth, Landa only elicited from the Indians the *word* which most approximated the sound of the Spanish word for "a," "b," "c," etc., thereby furnishing simply a collection of short words in no way related to an alphabet or even a phonetic system. (This illustrates one of the pitfalls of working with "native informants" who do not understand the purpose of the questions asked.) Brasseur de Bourbourg, by working with this erroneous alphabet in the Mayan language, which he spoke, made a translation of part of the Codex Troano which has since greatly influenced Donnelly and others. Here is the translation: "On the Sixth year of Can, in the Eleventh Muluc of the month of Zac, occurred dreadful earthquakes and continued until the Thirteenth Chuen. The Land of Clay Hills Mu and the Land of Moud were victims. They were shaken twice and in the night suddenly disappeared. The earth-crust was continually raised and lowered in many places by the subterranean forces until it could not resist such stresses, and many countries became separated from one another by deep crevices. Finally both provinces could not resist such tremendous stresses and sank in the ocean together with 64,000,000 inhabitants. It occurred 8,060 years ago."

Augustus Le Plongeon, another French archaeologist who spoke Maya, an explorer and excavater of Mayan cities, also, after Brasseur de Bourbourg, attempted a translation of the same materials as follows: "In the year 6 Kan, on the 11th Muluc in the month Zac, there occurred terrible earthquakes, which continued without interruption until the thirteenth Chuen. The country of the hills of mud, the land of Mu was sacrificed: being twice upheaved it suddenly disappeared during the night, the basin being continually shaken by the volcanic forces. Being confined, these caused the land to sink and to rise several times in various places. At last the surface gave way and ten countries were torn asunder and scattered. Unable to stand the force of the convulsion, they sank with their 64,000,000 of inhabitants 8060 years before the writing of this book."

In addition he tried an interpretive translation based on the old hieratic Egyptian system of hieroglyphics on the Xochicalco pyramid near Mexico City. His resultant translation was "A land in the ocean is destroyed and its inhabitants killed in order to transform them into dust. . . ."

These "translations" by Brasseur and Le Plongeon were frequently quoted and were certainly known to Donnelly. One wonders how dedicated scholars who took the trouble to learn American Indian languages and actively explored the jungle ruins of the Mayan Empire would purposely mistranslate inscriptions for personal gain or fame. Perhaps they did not *consciously* mistranslate them but simply interpreted them according to the thesis they were trying to prove. In other words, they saw in the inscriptions what they wanted to see—a phenomenon not necessarily restricted to Atlantologists.

To this day, however, none of the Mayan manuscripts or inscriptions have been successfully translated, although Russian archaeologists are reported to be working on breaking the Mayan system of writing through the use of computers.

Lewis Spence, a Scotch student of mythology, who wrote five books on Atlantis from 1924 to 1942, suggests not one Atlantis but two; one where Plato said it was and another part of it near the Antilles (called Antillia) in the vicinity of the present Sargasso Sea. He is joined in this general opinion of several Atlantic land masses by several other theorists on the subject who have assumed that Atlantis did not sink all at once, but submerged in a series of cataclysms separated in time, in a general reshaping of the earth's land surface that is still going on today.

Spence devoted much of his research to comparative mythology, especially in connecting the pre-Columbian legends of the American tribes and nations with legends of the ancient world, not only of the Mediterranean cultures but also those of the Celtic north, which as a Scotch mythologist he was amply qualified to represent.

From his vantage point Spence brings forth so many points of coincidence between these legends that one is easily convinced that either there was considerable communication between the Old and New Worlds before Columbus, or that each hemisphere obtained their legends from a central point, now vanished. As a single example—consider the similarities he points out between Quetzalcoatl, the Toltec god who brought civilization to Mexico and who went back to Tlapallan, his original home in the eastern sea—and Atlas, so important in the memory legends of Atlantis. The father of Atlas was Poseidon, Lord of the Sea while the father of Quetzal-coatl was Gucumatz, a diety of the ocean and earthquake—"the old serpent . . . who lives in the depth of the ocean." Quetzalcoatl and Atlas were each one of twins, both were represented as bearded and *each holds up the sky*.

One especially interesting aspect of Spence's theories on Atlantis concerns the waves of cultural immigration which apparently struck Europe *from the west* at certain periods, especially at about 25,000 B.C., 14,000 B.C. and 10,000 B.C., the latter date almost meshing with the supposed sinking of Atlantis.

These types of prehistoric European cultures have been given the names of the localities where such evidences were first discovered, Crô-Magnon or Aurignacian, the name of the oldest, having been first found at Crô-Magnon and also in a grotto of Aurignacin, both in southwestern France. From the Pyrenees region and from the Bay of Biscay this surprisingly advanced culture of more than 25,000 years ago spread through sections of southwestern Europe and Northern Africa and the Eastern Mediterranean. They left paintings and engravings on cave walls which imply a developed and sophisticated culture with an advanced knowledge of anatomy. These cave paintings or bas-reliefs demonstrate a preoccupation with the bull, which played an important role in Plato's account of Atlantean religion, as well as in the civilization of Crete and Egypt, with its sacred bull, Apis. Even today, although no longer a religious symbol, the bull is still, after 25,000 years. an important element in Spanish culture.

Crô-Magnon skulls indicate a much higher brain capacity than the then inhabitants of Europe—almost as if they were a race of supermen.

The Magdalenian culture of about 16,000 years ago is interpreted by Spence as a second wave of Atlantean immigration which contributed outstanding examples of painting, sculpture and carving as well as indications of a well formed tribal and religious organization. This second wave also came to Europe from the west or southwest.

The third or Azilian-Tardenoisian wave (named from the finds at Mas d'Azil, France, and Tardenos, Spain) of about 11,500 years ago were, according to Spence, the ancestors of the Iberians who spread into Spain and other parts of the Mediterranean, such as the Atlas Mountains. The Azilians buried their dead facing westward, apparently to the point from which they came.

The ancient Iberians were even referred to by the inhabitants of Italy in Roman times as "Atlanteans." Spence quotes Bodichon who observed: "The Atlanteans passed among the ancients as the favorite children of Neptune (Poseidon). They made (his) worship known to other nations—to the Egyptians for example. In other words, the Atlanteans were the first known navigators. . . ."

The Crô-Magnon, Magdalenian and Azilian cultures are facts, not theories. Spence has made an interesting contribution to the study of Atlantis by tying in the approximate dates attributed to the appearance of these cultures to flights of immigrants from Atlantis as a result of periodic submersions either caused by volcanic activity, flooding occasioned by the melting ice sheets of the glacial period, or a combination of both.

As these different cultures each appeared suddenly at different epochs in southwestern Europe, they must therefore have come from somewhere else and the spread eastward from the Biscay-Pyrenees region indicates that they came from the west, ostensibly from a land in the ocean.

The last culture, the Azilian, seems to have had, in addition to an unusual "geometric" form of art, a sort of writing or symbols written on stones, pebbles and bones. What may have been a living relic of these cultures was found in the Canary Islands in the fourteenth century. The Guanches were white, resembled the Crô-magnons in stature, worshipped the sun, had a highly developed stone-age culture and a system of writing, and conserved a legend of a universal catastrophe, of which they were the survivors.

Their discovery by Europeans proved, unfortunately for the Guanches, a more definitive catastrophe, one which they did not long survive. In writing of the concurrence in time between the reported sinking of Atlantis and the last appearance of prehistoric culture in Europe, Spence says: ". . . The fact that the date of the coming of the Azilian-Tardenoisians, as given by the best authorities, synchronizes generally with the date Plato gives for the destruction of Atlantis may be purely coincidental." However he goes on to explain that "some coincidences are more extraordinary than proven facts."

In general Spence expanded Donnelly's theories but somewhat downgraded Atlantis to a "stone-age" civilization, somewhat similar to that of ancient Mexico and Peru, but responsible for the Atlantean "culture complex" some of whose remains are still evident in the Atlantic area.

Spence, in his later years, became somewhat obsessed with the tradition recurring in so many legends as well as in the bible concerning the world before the flood, that the Atlanteans had been destroyed by divine displeasure because of their wickedness. In 1942, during World War II he published his last Atlantean

book entitled, appropriately enough under the circumstances—
*Will Europe Follow Atlantis?*

He also suggested that one reason for the durability of the
Atlantis theory was that a common "race memory" of the existence
of Atlantis could be inherited somewhat similarly, perhaps, to that
attributed to the flocks of birds that still seem to look for lost
Atlantis as a stopping place as they fly across the ocean on their
annual migration.

Other theories on Atlantis postulate that certain ancient cultures definitely known to have existed, such as that of the west
coast of Spain, North Africa, West Africa or the Mediterranean
islands such as Crete (and recently, Thera) were each, according to
the person doing the research, the real Atlantis and the reason for
the Atlantean tradition.

Some of these theories do not necessarily negate that of Atlantis—as the very existence of these extremely old and little known
cultural centers might be explained as having had their origin as
Atlantean colonies or places of refuge.

Tartessos is one of the principal "substitutes" for Atlantis. It is
thought to have been located on the Atlantic coast of Spain, at or
near the mouth of the Guadalquivir River, or perhaps where the
mouth of the river once was. It was the center of a highly developed and prosperous culture, especially rich in minerals. Tartessos
was captured by the Carthaginians in 533 B.C. and subsequently
sealed off from the rest of the world.

German archaeologists, especially Professors Schulten, Jessen,
Herman and Hennig, started their research on Tartessos as early as
1905. With a true Germanic sense of order Jessen set up in table
form "proof" that Tartessos, the "Venice of the West" was the
model of Plato's Atlantis.

Jessen lists eleven points to prove his thesis, comparing what Plato said and what Schulten, he and others had found or concluded about Tartessos. In abridged form his principal points are:

| What Plato Said | Facts (and Assumptions) about Tartessos |
|---|---|
| 1. Atlantis was in front of the Pillars of Hercules. | 1. Tartessos was an island in the mouth of the Guadalquivir River (past the Pillars of Hercules—Gibraltar.) |
| 2. It was bigger than Libya and Asia Minor. | 2. It was not an island, but a huge trade monopoly. |
| 3. It was a bridge to other islands and to the continent situated on the other side surrounded by the great ocean. | 3. Participants in the tin trade with Britain and other islands gave rise to the idea that Tartessos was a continent. |
| 4. Its empire extended over Africa to Egypt and to Etruria (in Italy). | 4. Tartessos supplied metals to all the Mediterranean. |
| 5. It vanished in a single day, submerged in the sea. | 5. It disappeared through conquest leaving no trace evident to Greek seafarers. |
| 6. The sea (over it) is inaccessible and cannot be explored. | 6. Inaccessible because of political reasons. |
| 7. Thick mud impedes navigation. | 7. Carthaginian propaganda. |
| 8. The land had rich mineral deposits. | 8. The Sierra Morena was one of antiquity's richest mineral deposits. |
| 9. There existed in Atlantis an extensive net of canals such as | 9. From the Guadalquivir a considerable net of canals radi- |

**What Plato Said—cont'd**

**Facts (and Assumptions) about Tartessos—cont'd**

was never seen in Europe.
10. The Atlantean king was the oldest of the people.

11. There were many ancient written laws in Atlantis, formed, it is said, 8,000 years ago.

ated, as mentioned by Strabo.
10. The last king of Tartessos, Arganthonios, reigned for 80 years.

11. Strabo * says of the Tudetanians (Tartessians) "They are the most civilized of the Iberians. They know writing and have ancient books, and also poems and laws in verse which they consider 7,000 years old."

* Strabo, a Greek geographer and historian (63 B.C.–21 A.D.).

Hennig, Schulten and other German scholars considered Tartessos to be not an Atlantean but a German colony, basing their supposition partly on Baltic amber found in the vicinity of Tartessos and partially on the theories of another German scholar with the unusual name of Redslob, who predicated widespread ocean navigation by prehistoric Germanic tribes.

Tartessos itself has not been definitely located, although large building blocks have been found underground in silted soil, too near the water level for practical excavation. (Do we hear an echo of Plato's account of the mud that impeded navigation?) The remains of Tartessos may be either under the sea or, covered by silt, under the land itself.

Mrs. E. M. Wishaw, directress of the Anglo-Spanish-American School of Archaeology and author of *Atlantis in Andalusia*, studied the area for 25 years. She believes, because of her discovery of a "sun temple" 27 feet beneath the streets of Seville, that Tartessos may be buried under the present day city. Actually much of ancient Rome is buried under modern Rome, Tenochtitlán is under the old section of Mexico City, and Herculaneum is under Resina, to mention only a few cases where archaelogists would like to pull down the present to get at the past.

Certain other remains connected with the culture of Tartessos can be observed in the Río Tinto copper mines, estimated at 8,000 to 10,000 years old, as well as the hydraulic engineering works near Ronda and an inland harbor at Niebla (which reminds one again of Plato's descriptions of the hydraulic works of Atlantis).

Far from agreeing with the German researchers that Tartessos itself gave rise to the Atlantis legend, Mrs. Wishaw believed that Tartessos was simply a colony of the real Atlantis. She wrote: "My theory, to sum it up concisely, is that Plato's story is corroborated from first to last by what we find here, even the Atlantean name of his son Gadir who inherited that part of Poseidon's kingdom beyond the Pillars of Hercules and ruled at Gades (Cadiz). . . ." And again: ". . . The marvellously civilized prehistoric people whose civilization I have put on record sprang from the fusion of the prehistoric Libyans, who in an earlier stage of the history of humanity came to Andalusia from Atlantis to purchase the gold, silver and copper provided by the neolithic miners of Río Tinto, and in the course of generations . . . welded the Iberian and African cultures so closely together that eventually Tartessos and Africa had a race in common, which was the Liby-Tartessian."

Tartessos was reputed to have written records going back 6,000 years. What is thought to be an excellent example of the written language is the inscription on a ring found (by Schulten) in a Spanish fishing village near Tartessos.

Mrs. Wishaw has compiled other pre-Roman Iberian inscrip-

Λ૮Ѵ૮૧ Ѵ૧ OF⟨Λ⟨⟨) Ѵ᠑Λ

Ѵ() Ѵ⟨૮.Ѵ() ⟨Λ ૧Ѵ() Ѵ⟨ ⟨

As yet untranslated "letters" found on a ring near the site of Tartessos.

tions (which no one has yet been able to translate) and finds that about 150 of these alphabetic signs also occur on the walls of the rock caverns of Libya.

Whether or not this proves the existence of Atlantis it does seem to establish the existence of a little known Western Mediterranean civilization of a very early period.

Many aspects of this culture resemble that of ancient Crete, which may have been related to it or had contacts with it. One of the most remarkable finds of the Iberian culture is the bust called "La Dama de Elche" (the Lady of Elche) found at Elche in southern Spain. This statue, which has sometimes been thought to portray a priestess of Atlantis, constitutes in itself a proof of the high civilization attained by the ancient inhabitants of Spain.

It has been frequently suggested that Scheria, the land "at the end of the world" of the Phaecians, described by Homer in the *Odyssey*, served Plato as a model for Atlantis. Many items descriptive of Scheria remind one of Plato's account of Atlantis; the marvelous and resplendent palace of Alcinoüs, "built on brass," the "gigantic city walls surprising to see," the sea power of the Phaecians, the city built on a plane with great mountains to the north, and even the mention of two springs in the royal garden.

The site of Scheria itself has remained in doubt. Homer, in telling of the land or island visited by Ulysses in his voyage with frequent and prolonged stop-overs home from the Trojan War, may have been retelling descriptions he had heard of anyone of several centers which had detained an early highly-developed civilization, such as Crete, Corfu, Tartessos, Gades, or, as suggested by Donnelly, Atlantis itself.

However, since the name Scheria occurs only in the *Odyssey*, the answer may lie in the meaning of the name, if it has any. As *schera* meant "trade" or "commerce" in Phoenician, the word could have been used simply as a general term for any lesser-known center of commerce of the era, and could therefore refer to far-western centers, such as Tartessos or Gades, or islands or an island continent in the Atlantic Ocean.

Other intriguing theories suggest that Atlantis never sank at all —that it is still on dry land and all we have to do is to dig for it. One important "dry land" theory is based on climactic changes in North Africa. Cave paintings 10,000 years old in the Tassili Mountains of Algeria and the connected Accasus chain of Libya depict a pleasant, populated, fertile land of rivers and forests, teeming with all kinds of African animals once present but now vanished from an area as barren, at the present day, as the surface of the moon. Besides the indications of a complete climactic change suggested by the cave paintings we see in their execution resemblances to those of prehistoric Europe, bearing witness to a developed culture and a long preparatory period of artistic development as indicated by the use of perspective and freeness of form. The presence of now-vanished game and a former large population fits in with the generally accepted theory that where there is now desert large inland rivers and forests once existed and even inland seas. Rem-

African cave paintings showing an amazingly sophisticated form of art, done by some race thousands of years back in pre-history. It is especially interesting to note that the original artist, with a highly developed sense of line and perspective, pictured the animals as a decorative study, peacefully grazing, while the crude hunting figure, a part of which is seen here, was added thousands of years later.

nants of these water courses still flow under the desert and the desert tribes still conserve the memory of more fertile lands. The gradual drying up of present day North Africa as well as the subsidence of much of the coast are the basis of other French theories predicating that both Tunisia and Algeria possessed an inland Sea, opening to the Mediterranean and also connecting with the inner Sahara Sea. The inland sea of Tunisia is associated with Lake Tritonis, mentioned by several classical writers, which lost its water when the dikes burst during an earthquake and eventually dried up, becoming the present Shott el Djerid, a marshy shallow lake in Tunisia.

The Sahara itself is considered to be the bed of an ancient sea, part of the ocean. In Algeria and Tunisia geodectic surveys made by the French government showed that the depression formed by the Shotts (shallow marshy lakes) of Algeria and Tunisia were below sea level and would fill up with water if a series of protective coastal dunes were removed.

The French archaeologist Godron, as early as 1868 proposed a theory that Atlantis was buried in the Sahara. The French geographer Etienne Berlioux, in 1874, also favored locating Atlantis in Africa but postulated that the real Atlantis was in North Africa in the Atlas Mountains, opposite the Canary Islands.

He thought that Cerne, the city mentioned by the ancient writer Diodorus Siculus as capital of the Atlantioi, was approximately at this very point. (Cerne has another historical mention through a voyage by the Carthaginian navigator Hanno which ended at a place of this name. Cerne is so indicated on some of the maps of Columbus' time.)

Berlioux, in his study of racial types, underlined a fact that the Berbers of the Atlas Mountains often have white skin, blue eyes and blond hair, denoting a Celtic (or Atlantean) origin. Later French writers have occasionally endorsed this point as possible justification for the Celtic Europeans (i.e., the French) taking control of North Africa. However, since they no longer have control, the point is moot.

P. Borchard, a German writer, in 1926 also adopted the North African theory and thought the capital of Atlantis was located in the Ahagger Mountains, home of the blue-veiled Turareg tribesmen, a vanishing race of mysterious origin (like the Berbers) who possess their own written language.

In considering the Berbers as possible relics of the Atlantean

North Africans, Borchard attempted to trace in the names of existing Berber tribes the names of the ten sons of Posiedon, that is, the clans of Atlantis. He found two unusual coincidences: one; that a Berber tribe was called *Uneur,* which fitted perfectly with *Euneor,* mentioned by Plato as the first inhabitant of Atlantis, and that the Berber tribes of the Shott el Hameina in Tunisia were called "Sons of the Source—*Attala.*"

The French archaeologists Butavand and Jollcaud subscribed to this theory but also place a large part of the Atlantean empire as sunken land off Tunis in the Gulf of Gabès. François Roux shares the belief that in prehistoric times North Africa was a fertile peninsula: ". . . the true Atlantis, traversed by many rivers and densely populated by men and animals. . . ." In his research Roux neatly tied together North African prehistoric culture to that of France, Spain and Portugal with the discovery of certain "stone age" pebbles and shards bearing symbols he considered to be writing. (See page 166.)

In considering fairly modern theories of Atlantis and its location, one is struck by the somewhat "nationalistic" character of the investigations, especially in the 20th century. Many of the French investigators searched for Atlantis in French North Africa and several authorities have indicated France itself as a possible location. Spanish archaeologists have tried to find it in Spain or in Spanish North Africa, while a Catalan writer declared it was in Catalonia. One Portuguese researcher, as if the Portuguese Azores are not enough, has declared that Atlantis was Portugal itself. Russian scientists think they have located Atlantis under the Caspian Sea or perhaps near Kerch, in the Crimea, while German scientists and archaeologists claim to have located it under the North Sea, in Mecklenberg, or as Tartessos, a "German Colony" in

Spain. (One large German book on the subject is entitled *Atlantis —Original Homeland of the Aryans*.) Irish and English writers have located "Plato's Island" as Ireland and England respectively; a Venezuelan specialist thinks that Atlantis was in Venezuela and a Swedish scholar claims to have located it in Upsala, Sweden.

At the present writing, Greek archaeologists think that the Atlantis legend can be traced to the island of Thera, which exploded about 1500 B.C. when a large part of it sunk beneath the Aegean Sea. Before the candidacy of Thera as a possible Atlantis, Crete, because of its surprisingly developed early civilization, sudden demise and presence of volcanic ash and signs of fire in its ruins, had also been considered by numerous scholars as the main reason for the Atlantis tradition. It is evident, however, that the volcanic eruption and earthquake that destroyed Thera may have affected Crete as well and that both of these cultures may have been destroyed by the same cataclysm.

Karst, a German orientalist, philologist and theorist on Atlantis, considerably expanded the problem of the location of Atlantis when he devised a theory of a double Atlantis—one in the west extending through North Africa, Spain and the Atlantic, and one in the east in the Indian Ocean, south of Persia and Arabia. In addition he detailed sub-focal points of regional civilization in the Altai Mountains of Asia and other regions, all of which he links together by the ties of language, names of places, tribes and peoples.

Faced with this multiplicity of "Atlantises" Bramwell, a neutral but excellent writer on the subject, astutely summarizes the problems of the many theories about where Atlantis really was when he suggests in his book *Lost Atlantis* that Atlantis must be considered either as an island in the Atlantic "or it is not Atlantis at all." In any case, the multiple prehistoric cultural foci around the Mediterranean, in western and northern Europe and the Americas do not necessarily constitute a substitute or replacement for Atlantis. On the contrary, any, many or even all of them *could* be vestiges of Atlantean colonization, just as Donnelly suggested.

A good case in point is the mysterious Yoruba or Ife culture of Nigeria of about 1600 B.C. The explorer Leo Frobenius, after considerable study of this unusual African culture, and finding in it what he considered certain similarities with Plato's account, stated: "I believe therefore to have found Atlantis again, center of a . . . . civilization, situated beyond the Pillars of Hercules, Atlantis, which Solon told us . . . that it was covered by flourishing vegetation, that fruitful plants furnished food, drink and medicine, that it produced the quickly-corrupted-fruit tree (the banana) and agreeable spices (pepper), that there were elephants there, that the country produced copper and that the dwellers wore clothes of deep blue. . . ."

Frobenius further based his theory of Atlantis-Nigeria on ethnological symbolism, that is use of symbols in common with other tribes, including, among other symbols, the swastica, worship of the sea god Olokun, tribal organization, types of artifacts, utensils, tools and weapons, tatooing, sexual rites and burial customs. In his comparisons he produced many unexpected similarities to other cultures including the Etruscan, prehistoric Iberian, Libyan, Greek and Assyrian. Although he claimed to have found Atlantis, Frobenius thought the Yoruba culture had originally come from the Pacific, through south Asia and across Africa. In claiming that he had found Atlantis therefore, he apparently meant that he had found what the ancient writers were referring to when they spoke of Atlantis—a mysterious civilization beyond the Pillars of Hercules.

This last instance illustrates the understandable tendency for an explorer or archaeologist to seek to associate a little-known culture which he has "discovered" with the concept of Atlantis, especially if the culture center is on, near, or under the sea. As the boundaries of prehistory are being pushed further and further back the time may not be far away when we will find whether true civilization originated in one place or in several; whether there was a large Atlantic island whose influence spread to the other continents or whether the unusual resemblances among prehistoric civilizations was merely a fortuitious coincidence.

# 9 Atlantis and the Establishment

Aristotle, a former pupil and later the founder of a school of philosophy in competition with Plato, seized upon the abrupt ending of Plato's account of Atlantis as conclusive proof that Atlantis had existed solely in Plato's inventive mind. In referring specifically to the abrupt ending to Plato's account, Aristotle observes succinctly: "He who made it (Atlantis) destroyed it." Aristotle thereby established himself as the first in a long line of distinguished sceptics on the subject of Atlantis in a polemic which has come down through and survived the intervening centuries and millenia.

The established academic historical community and to a somewhat lesser degree the scientific world, has long regarded the question of Atlantis with scepticism, disbelief and even a certain amount of hilarity. Scholars of history are naturally less than enthusiastic about "intuitive history" based on "race memory," which is the basis of a great deal of writing about Atlantis. In addition,

serious consideration of the Atlantis theory, even based on what
has already been discovered, would cause a number of established
tenets concerning early civilization to tumble, with considerable
rewriting of our early history. However, with new archaeological
techniques for excavating on land, in swamps, or underwater, re-
storing and especially for dating, much of the mystery of Atlantis
may be solved in the not too distant future.

Whether one accepts the theory of Atlantis or not, study of the
problem has almost a hypnotic effect, not only on those interested
in establishing Atlantis' existence but also on those dedicated to
proving that Atlantis is a dream or a hoax. For example, one of the
best and most complete Spanish books on Atlantis concludes that
study of the problem is a waste of time, notwithstanding the years
of research dedicated to the subject by the author himself. Some
"Anti-Atlantean" books of this type, in detailed examination of
sources and theories, have sometimes inadvertently come up with
additional evidence which reinforces the Atlantis theory.

The fact remains, however, that the established world of research and history remains unconvinced, for lack of more concrete
proof. But modern partisans of Atlantis have an answer to this in
the great partisan of the nineteenth century—Donnelly—when he
says: "For a thousand years it was believed that the legends of the
buried cities of Pompeii and Herculaneum were myths: they were
spoken of as 'the fabulous cities.' For a thousand years the edu-
cated world did not credit the accounts given by Herodotus of the
wonders of the ancient civilizations of the Nile and of Chaldea. He
was called "the father of liars." Even Plutarch sneered at him.
Now, ". . . the deeper and more comprehensive the researches of
the moderns have been, the more their regard and esteem for
Herodotus has increased. . . ."

Donnelly also points out that the Egyptian circumnavigation of Africa under the Pharaoh Necho was doubted because of the fact that the explorers reported that the sun was north of them after some time of sailing down the coast, indicating that they had passed the equator; in other words, the very proof of their voyage was the cause of subsequent disbelief. (But it now proves to us that the Egyptian navigators had anticipated by more than 2100 years the discovery of the cape of Good Hope by Vasco da Gama.)

To these examples of Donnelly numerous others could be added —the disbelief in the existence of the gorilla and the okapi before specimens of these "mythical" animals were obtained as well as, relatively recently, the "dragon" lizards of Komodo. In the field of science one among many contested beliefs comes to mind; the possibility of transmuting metals, a point where the efforts of alchemists throughout the ages has now been proved possible by modern science.

In archaeology, besides the vindication-by-discovery of Pompeii and Herculaneum, one may also point out the widespread doubt that once existed about reports of "lost Indian cities" in the jungles of Central America, before their discovery in the 19th century and subsequent archaeological furor. Moreover, Persian, Babylonian and Assyrian inscriptions in the Middle East were long thought not to be writing at all, but decorations, until they were deciphered and furnished a detailed history of an area which the native inhabitants at that time had completely ignored or forgotten.

Perhaps the most outstanding of all proofs by discovery in archaeology was that of Heinrich Schliemann who, in 1871, discovered Troy, or at least a series of superimposed cities on the supposed site of Troy at Hissarlik, in Turkey, although Troy too had been long considered something of a myth. Schliemann had been influenced as a young boy by a lithograph of the Trojan War, showing the huge walls of Troy, which he could not believe had vanished completely because of their size. He continued his studies of Homeric times throughout a successful business career which he abandoned in 1863 to find Troy, which he did, mainly basing his quest on the classical written material available, giving a tremendous impetus to modern archaeology. Subsequently he made important discoveries at Mycenae and elsewhere, although he has been criticized by some students for being too hasty in establishing his certainly important finds as the immediate object of his search. For example, the beautiful golden mask of Agamemnon of Mycenae is certainly someone's golden death mask, but whether it was Agamemnon's or not is still open to discussion.

By an unusual series of events, the activities of a grandson of this famous and intuitive archaeologist have brought considerable discredit upon the theory of Atlantis. Paul Schliemann, in an article written for the Hearst newspapers in 1912, claimed that his grandfather, who had long been interested in the subject of Atlantis, shortly before his death in 1890 had left a sealed letter to be opened by someone in his family who would devote his life to the investigations indicated in the letter.

Also, Paul alleged that an hour before his death his grandfather had added an unsealed postscript with the instructions: "Break the owl-headed vase. Examine the contents. It concerns Atlantis." Paul wrote that he did not open the letter, which had been deposited with a French bank, until 1906. When he did finally open it he learned that his grandfather had found in his excavations of Troy a bronze vase containing some clay tablets, metal objects, coins and petrified bones, with the inscription on the vase reading in Phoenician writing: "From King Chronos of Atlantis."

According to Paul Schliemann his grandfather had examined a vase from Tihuanaco and found in it pottery shards of the same chemical composition as well as metal objects of an identical amalgam of platinum, aluminium and copper. He became convinced that these diverse objects were linked by a central point of origin—Atlantis; and, according to Paul Schliemann, he continued his very productive investigations, finding several papyrus manuscripts in St. Petersburg concerning Egyptian prehistory and one concerning an Egyptian sea search for Atlantis. He conducted these investigations in secret (although in truth this would be rather atypical of Heinrich Schliemann) until his death.

The younger Schliemann wrote that he conducted his own investigations before returning to Paris and breaking open the owl-headed vase, in which he found a four-angled white metal disk, much wider than the neck of the vase, "on one side of which strange signs and figures were engraved, which resemble nothing I ever saw either of hieroglyphics or writing." On the other side was an archaic Phoenician inscription: ". . . having come from the temple of transparent walls." Among other pieces in his grandfather's collection Paul allegedly found a ring of the unknown amalgam, a statuette of an elephant carved from petrified bone, as well as a map used by an Egyptian navigator in a search for Atlantis. (Could he have borrowed it from the St. Petersburg Museum during his investigations?) Pursuing his own investigations in Egypt and Africa, Paul Schliemann found other objects of the mysterious metal which caused him to suggest that he had five links in a chain: "The coins of the secret collection of my grandfather, the coin from the vase from Atlantis, the coins from the Egyptian sarcophagus, the coin from the Central American vase, and the child's head (of metal) of the Moroccan Coast."

A neutral observer might equate Paul Schliemann's preoccupation with finding mysterious coins with an understandable desire to acquire more modern currency, especially since he first sold his story to a newspaper chain, and subsequently none of his finds stood up under investigation. His closing words in his statement of his discoveries are: "But if I wanted to say everything that I know, there would be no more mystery," surely one of the most unusual statements in the history of scientific investigation.

Claims made or offered by an individual based on relics or artifacts that can be touched or examined are still within the scientific frame of reference that can be accepted or rejected by the establishment, historical or scientific. But much Atlantean research has been channeled in other directions, including that of collective race memory, recollections based on reincarnation, inherited memory and even spiritualism. Such research is necessarily both outside the scope of academic research and beyond its reach. Such spiritual or non-physical approaches to Atlantis from various sources have elicited a variety of information, some of which agrees with general Atlantean theories and some of which is surprisingly different.

Edgar Cayce, an example of the above category, was a clairvoyant prophet and psychic researcher who died in 1945 but whose collection of "psychic interviews" have since become the nucleus for the Edgar Cayce Foundation—the Association for Research and Englightenment. This association with headquarters in Virginia Beach and Centers in several American cities as well as one in Tokyo, has certain characteristics of a movement, one in which the study of Atlantis occupies an important place.

Cayce's interviews are the result of personal memories of former incarnations and those of other individuals "read" by Cayce.

About 700 psychic interviews given by Cayce over the years in answer to questions while in a state of trance deal specifically with happenings in history in the time of Atlantis, as well as predictions, as in the case of the underwater "Atlantean" temple off Bimini, of discoveries yet to come. One especially interesting future find will be the discovery of an underground chamber of Atlantean records which will precede the reemergence of Atlantis. The sealed chamber will eventually be found by following lines of shadows made by the morning sun falling between the paws of the Sphinx.

In the Cayce readings Atlantis is traced down from its beginnings to its Golden Age, with its great stone cities which enjoyed all forms of modern advantages including mass communication, land, air and undersea transportation, and some that we have not yet attained such as the neutralization of gravity and the harnessing of the sun's energy through electric crystals or "fire stones." Misuse of these crystals caused two of the cataclysms that eventually destroyed Atlantis. Unlike in our own times, there was a connection between material inventions and spiritual force, as well as a closer understanding and communication with animals, until materialism and perversion ended the Golden Age.

The deterioration of Atlantean civilization, according to Cayce's readings, made its final destruction all the more certain. These factors included civil discontent, the enslavement of workers and "mixtures" (the offspring of human and animal interbreeding), conflict between the "Sons of the Law of One" and the depraved "Sons of Belial," human sacrifice, widespread adultery and fornication, and misuse of the forces of nature, especially the employment of the "fire stones" which were used for punishment and torture.

Other occult or psychic researchers, such as W. Scott Elliot,

Madame Blavatsky, and Rudolph Steiner all rely on occult sources or racial or inherited memory for their information. They hold a general opinion that Atlantis caused its own destruction because it became evil; an opinion shared not only by Spence and the Russian historian Merezhkowski, but also by Plato and the writers of Genesis and the other flood legends in the description of the wickedness of the world before the Flood.

In regard to Cayce's account of the deterioration or self-destruction of Atlantis it is sufficient to substitute the words "materialistic" for "evil" and "the bomb" for "the crystals" or "fire stones" and we get a rather pertinent message applicable to our own period from a time *before* the beginning of the atomic age.

Cayce's prophecies about the reemergence of Atlantis will be doubtful blessings if they come true, inasmuch as New York City "will in the main disappear" and the West Coast will be "broken up" and most of Japan "will go into the sea." New Yorkers, Californians and Japanese have therefore a vested interest in hoping that Cayce is wrong, although he has proved disturbingly right in several past predictions about race riots, Presidential deaths, and earthquakes in the Mississippi Valley.

As psychic research is not yet considered a reliable source for establishing the authority of history, the voluminous psychic material on Atlantis represents a section of Atlantean literature that elicits, at best, a "no comment" from the archaeological or scientific community.

Individuals united by a common belief and desire to establish proof of the former existence of Atlantis have frequently formed organizations whose activities have sometimes tended to weaken, rather than strengthen, popular acceptance of Atlantis as a historic entity. In France, between the two World Wars, Atlantean organizations flourished, such as *Les Amis d'Atlantis*—"The Friends of Atlantis"—founded by Paul le Cour, who also published a magazine called *Atlantis*. Another group called *Société d' Études Atlantéennes*—"Society for Altantean Studies"—received a physical as well as a moral setback when one of its meetings at the Sorbonne was broken up by tear gas bombs thrown by members apparently more in favor of an intuitive than a scientific approach to the question of Atlantis. The President of the Society, Roger Dévigne admitted in a later report that the Society "is affected by the discredit legitimately attached to these dreams in the eyes of the scientific world" and further mentions "prudent mistrust" inspired by the sight of members "wearing Atlantean emblems in their lapels on their way to Atlantean picnics. . . ."

The writings of other Atlantologists, however, have undergone a close and generally disapproving scrutiny under the microscopes of the "establishment." Even the imaginative and visionary style of books about Atlantis is annoying to scientific archaeologists who prefer matter-of-fact theories, without the addition of poetry. For, as the "Lost Continent" is such a romantic theme, poets have long used it as an inspiration and, as they are quoted in most books on Atlantis, the impression given to the subject is more one of fantasy than fact.

While neutral on the subject of Atlantean poetry, the anti-Atlantis writers are sometimes as positive in their assaults on the possibility of there ever having been an Atlantis as the adherents of Atlantis are positive that it existed. For example, a proof of no Atlantis is presented in the report of Dr. Ewing of Columbia University who "spent thirteen years exploring the mid-Atlantic ridge" but "found no trace of sunken cities." Isn't this a case of "looked for it and couldn't find it so it obviously doesn't exist?"

If the palaces and temples of Atlantis are lying broken and ruined on the floor of the Atlantic, they would be covered to a great extent by sedimentation and mud, and it would be somewhat difficult to find and recognize them after thousands of years, by a system of "spot checking." One might suggest an analogy of space travelers throwing down nets at random on the earth at night from their flying saucers, without seeing where they were throwing them, and after bringing them up empty of animals and people, concluding that there was no sentient life on earth.

Even the underwater cities of the Mediterranean have been discovered only comparatively recently and in relatively shallow water. Because of a general rising of the water level of the Mediterranean through classical times, large sections of cities well known to history are now under water and are currently being studied and excavated with new techniques specially developed by underwater archaeologists. These submerged cities or sections of cities include Baiae, a sort of ancient Las Vegas, as well as many other points along the western coast of Italy in the vicinity of Naples and the Adriatic coast of Yugoslavia, and also parts of Syracuse in Sicily, Leptis Magna in Libya, Cenchreae, the port of Corinth, in Greece, and the ancient harbors of Tyre and Caeserea, to mention only a few.

All sorts of surprising archaeological finds are still waiting to be uncovered. The camps that Hannibal used as a staging area prior to his invasion of Rome lie under shallow water off Peñíscola on t : eastern coast of Spain. Cousteau tells of finding a paved road un the bottom of the ocean far out in the Mediterranean, which he swam along until forced to surface, but could not find a second time. Helike sunk under the Gulf of Corinth in an earthquake, but remained visible on the bottom for hundreds of years. In fact it was a tourist attraction for Roman visitors to Greece, who would pass over it in boats, and admire the ruins visible through the clear water, especially the statue of Zeus which was still standing and clearly visible on the bottom. Helike which is now being searched for again, has since either subsided under the silt at the bottom of the Gulf or, because of seismatic changes, may now be under the land.

Sunken cities, real or imagined, are by no means all located in the Mediterranean. In India, off Mahabalipuram, Madras, there are remains of a sunken city now under investigation, and in the Gulf of Mexico near Cozumel there are underwater buildings of presumably Mayan origin. In the USSR a sunken city exists in the Bay of Baku and blocks of masonry bearing reliefs of animal carvings and inscriptions have been hauled up from its underwater walls.

Breton tradition places the sunken city of Ys fairly close to the French coast. The submergence of Ys was reputedly caused by Dahut, the daughter of Gradlon, King of Ys, who opened the floodgates of the city with a stolen key, during a drinking bout with her lover, to see what would happen. King Gradlon, forewarned, was able to escape to higher land ahead of the advancing waters on his galloping horse. Apart from its commentary on very early juvenile delinquency, this story probably refers to actual cases of settlements on the French coast that have been covered by the sea. Several years ago a tremendous ebb tide occurred off the coast of Brittany and, for a short time, piles of rocks, apparently constructions, were visible on the exposed sea bottom, but were covered again by the tide and the waters thereafter returned to their normal depth.

Attractive as this prospect of lost sunken cities in the Mediterranean and in other seas may be, what has it to do with Atlantis? There are several pertinent connections. A writer who has devoted a great deal of time to disproving Atlantis has suggested that land subsidence such as we see in the Mediterranean has been relatively slight within civilized times. Underwater research in the Mediterranean, however, is proving the contrary. An archaeologist who was looking for something else—namely, the arms of the Venus de Milo—on the sea floor near Melos in the Aegean, unexpectedly came upon ruins of a city extending as far as 400 feet below the surface, with roads branching out from it descending even deeper—to unknown destinations.

The underwater ruins lying on the floor of the Pacific off the coast of Peru, discovered by Dr. Menzies in 1966 at a depth of 6,000 feet, will furnish, when and if they can be studied, more conclusive proof of the extent of land sinkings within the period that man has been civilized enough to build cities.

Critics of the Atlantis concept believe its adherents are either visionaries or irresponsible; that Atlantis never existed; that land did not sink so much in historic times and finally, according to the theory of continental drift, that it could never have existed because there was no room for it in the continental pattern.

This last reference is concerned with the Wegener theory of continental drift, a theory that, whether or not one understands its implication or explanation, can at least be checked by anyone with access to a world map and a pair of scissors. For if you cut out each of the continents you will find that some of them fit neatly together like parts of a puzzle. This is especially noticeable in the case of the east coat of Brazil and the west coast of Africa, the east coast of Africa and the west coast of Arabia, the east coast of Greenland and the west coast of Norway. Even the types of rock and earth formation seem to be directly connected from one continent to the other, although separated by the ocean.

This phenomenon had been noticed by other geographers, including Humboldt, long before Alfred Wegener used it as a basis for his theory of continental drift. Wegener (who died in scientific action on the Greenland icecap in 1930 while testing his theories) thought that all continents were formerly combined in one single land mass which separated into continents and have ever since been drifting apart on the sima crust of the earth like enormous floating islands. Some land masses, such as Greenland, are thought to be moving more rapidly than others; one report noted that Greenland was continuing on its separate westward course at more than 50 feet a year. (One is reminded of the Norwegian lemmings

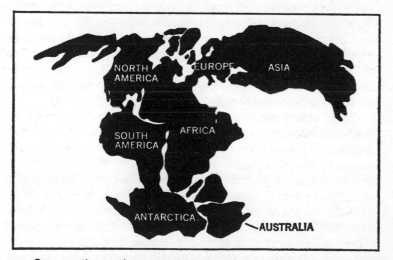

One way the continents would fit together in Wegener's Continental Drift Theory.

who have been cited as having an instinctive memory of Atlantis in their westward and suicidal swim. Perhaps they were simply trying to catch up with Greenland!)

If the theory of continental drift is correct, and all the continents can be fitted snugly back together, where does that leave Atlantis? The answer is, more or less where it was before because, although some of the continents fit quite exactly together, the fitting together of others would leave considerable gaps, especially in the section of the Atlantic where the underwater Mid Atlantic Ridge is the widest. In fact the whole Mid Atlantic Ridge is like a reflection of the shape pattern of the west boundary line of Europe, Africa and the east boundary line of the opposite Americas. Therefore, as the continents pulled apart, certain lands were perhaps left and later submerged along the break. So even in a theory that at first glance seems to negate the existence of Atlantis, its presence nevertheless still makes itself felt as the missing piece to complete the puzzle or solve the mystery.

In their task of demolishing the Atlantean concept its critics have been aided by the over-exuberance of some of its proponents, as well as certain evident errors in their reports. Donnelly and others, writing in an age when anthropology was relatively undeveloped, ascribed racial affinities to separate peoples which modern research has often disproved. In the field of language resemblances however, they are even more vulnerable. Le Plongeon, for example, (who spoke Maya) claimed that it was "one third pure Greek. Who brought the dialect (!) of Homer to America? Or who took to Greece that of the Mayas?" As Maya and Greek are still living languages, this was and is fairly easy to disprove. (Besides, as we have seen, Le Plongeon enthusiastically connects the Maya and Egyptian systems of writing which, except that they are both picture writing, have no noticeable connection.)

In like manner the Chiapanec of the Mexican Indians is said to be related to Hebrew (from the migration of the 10 lost tribes?); the Otomi Indian language to Chinese (because of its tonal qualities); and the almost forgotten Mandan Indian language to Welsh. Almost all Atlantean writers see in Farrar's reference to the Basque language in *Families of Speech* a proof of pre-Columbian language bridge to the Americas via Atlantis. He wrote: "There never has been any doubt that this isolated language, preserving its identity in a western corner of Europe, between two mighty kingdoms, resembles in its structure the aboriginal languages of the vast opposite continent (America) and those alone."

Donnelly, in showing relationships between widely separated languages compared word examples in various European and Asian languages which we now know to be related so that similarities between European languages and Sanskrit or Persian should surprise no one and certainly should not be considered in the study of Atlantis. However, since this connection was not known at that time, we may consider Donnelly a sort of linguistic pioneer, although a frequently incorrect one. In his quest for similarities between Chinese and Otomi, for example, he gives Chinese words that do not mean what he says they mean. Perhaps he obtained them, like Bishop Landa with the Mayan "alphabet" in Yucatan, from an obliging informant who simply did not understand his question, an occurrence not unfamiliar to linguists then or now.

In addition, Donnelly sometimes paints himself into a linguistic corner as in the case where he presents the word "hurricane" in different European and American languages as a proof of pre-Columbian diffusion. The word was the name of the Carib storm god Hurakán who caused hurricanes and it exists in English as "hurricane"; French as "ourigan"; in Spanish as "huracán"; in German as "Orkan," etc. But Donnelly failed to realize that it obviously never existed in these languages *before* the discovery of America and the unnerving experiences of European sailors in the tropical storms of the Caribbean.

Nevertheless, with all the evident hasty conclusions and frequent misinterpretations abounding in Atlantean lore, certain aspects are difficult to dismiss and underneath all the verbiage of support and dissent, one senses the presence of something more profound, a common memory of shared cultural and religious traditions, language and lost history, like the nine-tenths of the iceberg that lie beneath the water, as compared to the one tenth that we see on the surface. This may be why, like the resurgent phoenix that is constantly reborn, the Atlantis legend continues in waves of returning interest from one generation to the next and will most probably outlive its critics.

# 10 〰 Atlantis, Language and the Alphabet

What language did the Atlanteans speak? Is there any indication of an isolated language of great antiquity, having connection with other ancient languages which might be such a relic?

The answer is almost too easy—for such a language does exist, and present day Basques are happy to agree that they are descendents of the Atlanteans. It is generally considered that the ancient Iberians spoke Basque before the Celtic and subsequent Roman conquest, and Sprague de Camp, an outstanding modern researcher on Atlantis and author of one of the most complete books on the subject, *Lost Continents*, thinks that the inscription on the "Tartessos ring" may be written in the original Basque, before Basque adopted Roman letters.

Basque stands alone and unclassified among the languages of Europe and on closer inspection does not seem to be very close to the American Indian languages either, although it has *more* affinity with them than with the Indo-Germanic group, with which it has none at all. It's affinities are strange: Basque shares construction similarities with the other agglutinative languages such as Quechua (the language of the Incas) and the Ural-Altaic group—Finnish, Esthonian, Hungarian, Turkish. (These languages form very long words including articles and other working parts of speech.) But Basque also resembles the polysynthetic type of language—such as those of the American Indian, Eskimo, etc. whose linguistic peculiarity consists of complex words that are really sentences.

Certain Basque words seem to go back to the Crô-Magnon days of the cave paintings. The word for "ceiling" literally means "top of the cavern," while "knife" is formed of component words meaning "the stone that cuts." The antiquity of the Basques would seem to fit in well with Spence's theory of separate waves of Atlantean immigration to Spain and France with each partial sinking of Atlantis.

However Basque does not appear to have traceable influences on any other language or to be influenced by any other. It is an interesting relic of something else—perhaps a living fossil—a representative of the pre-glacial language of Europe or, even better, the only surviving remnant of the language of Atlantis.

Since, unlike Donnelly, we now know the many connections between the Indo-Germanic and Semitic languages, we no longer need to be astounded when words are traceable and recognizable in a number of quite different languages. What can still surprise us, however, is to find common words where no language or other communication existed, such as between Europe and pre-Columbian America.

As languages have a relatively small number of possible sound units (phonemes is the linguistic name for it), certain sound coincidences in non-related languages are likely to occur. In Japanese, for instance, the word "so" has the same meaning as the English "so," as in the sense of "that is so," and it is an indigenous word, not one imported since contact with the West.

Common words in widely separated languages would indicate either a linguistic or cultural relationship—or perhaps both. For this reason it is especially intriguing to find words of a spiritual level in American Indian languages which more or less closely resemble words of ancient languages across the Atlantic.

In Greek, *thalassa* was "the sea," and in Maya *thallac* means "not solid," while Tlaloc, the God of Water of the Aztecs was also connected with the sea. In Chaldean mythology Thalath was the goddess who ruled over chaos. *Atl* means "water" in Náhuatl (Aztec) and also in the Berber language of North Africa.

Other unusual coincidences include the consonance between the American Indian word for "great spirit"—*Manitu*—with the Hindu *Manu*; the Náhuatl word for "god"—*teo* (*théulh*)—with the Greek *théos*.

Other coincidences of words are less spiritual but none the less evocative. In Basque, *argi* is "light," while *arg* is Sanskrit for "brilliant." The Basque word for "dew" is *garúa*, while this same sound means "drizzle" in Quechua and has been adopted from Quechua into Spanish. *Tepec*, the Náhuatl word for "hill" is also "hill" in the Turkic languages of central Asia (*tepe*); and *malko*, a Central American word for "king," is easily recognizable in the Arabic *malik* or Hebrew *melek*. The Greek word for "river"—*potamos* finds a coincidental reflection not only in the Delaware Indian *potomac* but also in the *poti* for "river" of the Brazilian Indians of the Tupi Guarani language group.

Guarani, an Indian language of Paraguay and Southern Brazil has linguistic coincidences with apparently unrelated languages. To mention a few, *oka* means "home" in Guarani and *oika* is a word for "home" in Greek; and *ama*—"water" resembles the Japanese *ame*—"rain." In Quechua, the language of the Incas, "person" is *runa* while "person" or "man" in Chinese is *rhen*. *Anti* was "high valley" in ancient Egyptian and in Quechua *andi* is "high crest" or "ridge." And although it is perhaps onomatapaeic—in this case resembling the sound of a milk-giving animal—the Quechua word for "milk" is *ñu-ñu* (n'yoo-n'yoo) while the Japanese word for "milk" is *g'yu-n'yu*. The language of the small tribe of Mandan Indians, who formerly lived in Missouri and were practically exterminated by smallpox in 1838, possessed some startling similarities with Welsh. Some of them are:

|           | **Welsh**    | **Mandan** |
|-----------|--------------|------------|
| boat      | corwyg       | koorig     |
| paddle    | rhwyf (ree)  | ree        |
| old       | hen          | her        |
| blue      | glas         | glas       |
| bread     | barra        | bara       |
| partridge | chugjar      | chuga      |
| head      | pen          | pan        |
| great     | mawr         | mah        |

The similarity of the lost Mandan language to Welsh, however, may have a more direct explanation in the theory that the Mandans were descendents of the followers of the Welsh prince, Madoc, who sailed west from Wales in 1170 to found a colony in a western land and never returned.

But while some of the American Indian languages have certain linguistic coincidences in sound and meaning with transatlantic or transpacific languages, there is as yet no proof of much closer connection, except of course, with the tribes of Alaska and Siberia who were near enough to disregard natural or man-made boundaries. As for the others, it is perfectly possible that some words were exchanged by pre-Columbian explorers, like Madoc, or by travelers who lost their way, in either direction, like the "red skinned people" who suddenly appeared in a long canoe off the coast of Germany in the first century A.D. and who were enslaved and given as presents to the Roman proconsul of Gaul. These Indians, as they seem to have been, had no time to make any linguistic contributions, but the point of their having made the crossing in a long canoe tends to show how some pre-Columbian cultural and linguistic interchange could have been accomplished and of course, much more easily if there were intervening land on the way.

Apart from coincidences we should look for a clue—even a word—which would connect not one or two but many completely different and separated peoples, tribes and nations, and imply an earlier and deeper diffusion. It should be basic, fairly recognizable, and include, if possible, a suspected "Atlantean" language such as Basque, some American Indian languages as well as Indo-Germanic and other language groups.

A word like "mama," while it would fill these specifications, would have to be ruled out, since it is a sound apparently automatically uttered by children for "mother" in almost all languages. (There are always exceptions—in Ewe (West Africa) "mother" is *dada*, and in Georgian (the Caucasus) "mother" is *deda* while, unaccountably, "father" is *mama*.)

There exists, however, another word of great antiquity and in use in many languages, all located in different countries and even on islands of the ocean. It is not an automatic sound reflex but an individual word. Starting with Basque, note the similarity of the vowels and consonants in the translations of the word "father":

> Basque—aita
> Quechua—taita
> Turkish (and other Turkic languages)—ata
> Dakota (Sioux)—atey (até)
> Náhuatl—tata (or) tahtli
> Seminole—intáti
> Zuni—tachchu (tat'chu)
> Maltese—tata
> Tagalog—tatay
> Welsh—tàd
> Roumanian—tată
> Sinhalese—thàthà (tata)
> Fijian—tata
> Samoan—tata

One is struck by the primitive or ancient aspect of some of these languages, as well as their extensive distribution. There may be other words, dim traces of an antediluvian language, that one will be able to discover and recognize—further down the branches of the tree trunk from whose roots the original base language of humanity may have come, and of which the Romance, Germanic, Slavic, Sinictic and Semitic languages are only the upper branches.

But the languages related by this one word, except in the case of Turkish and Roumanian and possibly a revived Tagalog, seem to be linguistic islands, and most of them appear to be retracting under the pressure of modern languages and mass communication.

If traceable spoken words on a "prehistoric" level are difficult to locate, perhaps another key, a written one, would give a more concrete answer to the question of ethnic and linguistic diffusion across the Atlantic ocean and possibly refer in concrete form to the existence of a land bridge or to Atlantis. Such written records, however, have already brought considerable disrepute to Atlantean studies, notably in the cases of Paul Schliemann and the controversial "Phoenician" inscription in the owl headed vase, and Brasseur de Bourbourg with his interpretive translation, as well as James Churchward, an American, who based his theory of Atlantis in the Atlantic and another "lost continent," Mu, in the Pacific principally on "tablets" in India and Tibet which are not available for study by others.

Writing is a result of picture writing becoming simplified or formalized as in the case of hieroglyphic Egyptian or Chinese or evolved into a sort of mixed picture plus a syllabic alphabet as in the case of the ancient cuneiform of the Middle East.

All primitive tribes draw pictures and occasionally they draw them in almost the same way. Wirth, among others, has made exhaustive studies of the use of simple pictures and symbols, such as the cross, the swastika, rosettes, crossed circles, Y-shapes, etc., suggesting the relationship of picture writings with symbols, which he called "the sacred primitive writing of humanity." As proof of the theory of cultural diffusion from Atlantis which he held, he gives, among other examples, selected ancient drawings or incised carvings of ceremonial ships. Some of these show startling similarities, as if the artists at widely separated geographical ports had seen and drawn the same ships:

**Prehistoric and early representations of sacred ships, or "sun boats," found in widely separated areas such as Egypt, Sumeria, California, Spain, and Sweden.**

Spence also produces an example, showing that an American Indian primitive drawing of a buffalo contains a sign written on the buffalo almost identical with one discovered in a stone age cave of western Europe of the Aurignacian period:

Is the sign a form of writing meaning "buffalo"? Or is it the personal or clan name of the person hunting the buffalo? Or does it mean "I killed him," or was it a charm to make the hunter able to kill the buffalo, having first captured the spirit of the animal by making the drawing? We will probably never know, but can only wonder at the remarkable writing or symbolic coincidence between the America Indian and the cave culture of Europe.

The Aurignacian version is so primitive that it in no way compares with other more advanced Crô-Magnon, Magdalenian or Aurignacian pictures with their implication of an advanced artistic culture and therefore does not make any special contribution to the theory of Atlantean civilization. In like manner, Spence has pointed out, as part of his theory of Atlantean diffusion, the presence of hand prints on ancient cave paintings in Europe and America. This too fails to be much of a proof inasmuch as leaving a hand print of one's work can be termed an almost automatic reaction in prehistoric or historic times, or (in wet cement) even now.

Extremely ancient marks or geometric designs from the pre-gla-

Marks found in cave in Rochebertier, France, which may be picture writing, a talley, or even an alphabet. If the latter is true, a form of writing existed eight to ten thousand years before our present alphabet came into use.

cial caverns of France and Spain look like writing but may be simply crude picture-writing, tallies or property marks. Moreover, a collection of painted stones from the Mas d'Azil caves of France more than 12,000 years old, seem to have letters on them, an intriguing thought though hardly in accord with generally accepted theory about the origin of writing. (The Azilian culture, one recalls, was thought by Spence to be the third great migration from Atlantis at the time of the final sinking.)

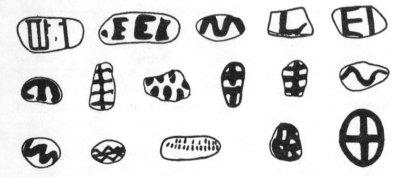

Signs on colored pebbles from Mas d'Azil, France. It is not known whether the signs are decorations or notations.

Egyptian hieroglyphs, a form of picture writing that evolved into a combination of pictures and syllables is perhaps the oldest form of developed writing that we have examples of. This writing was considered by the Egyptians to have been the language of the gods, a belief frequently interpreted by Atlantologists that the "gods" were the people from the Western Ocean who brought civilization to Egypt.

Systems of writing, first by pictures and then evolving into conventionalized pictures or signs to stand for syllables, have been invented in various parts of the world, apparently independently. The Sumerian cuneiform system of the ancient Middle East, that of pressing wedge-shaped lines into wet clay, also started with pictures and evolved into a syllabic system.

But the true alphabet, where a relatively small number of single letters compose words, seems to have originated among the Phoenicians as far back as 2000—1800 B.C. and spread out from the Mediterranean in all directions, forming a variety of different alphabets, all related, notwithstanding how different they look. All true alphabets in the world are considered to be related to the first basic one, usually labeled Phoenician because Phoenician traders were apparently the first ones to use it.

The alphabets used by the Phoenicians and other North Semitic groups evolved from a form of picture writing with A (aleph in Aramaic) standing for an ox, (you can still see the horns if you turn a capital A upside down), B (bet) meaning a house, D (dalet) meaning a door, G (gimmel or gamel) meaning a camel, etc. (Every time we say the word "alphabet" we pay tribute to its originators by repeating the two ancient Aramaic words for "ox" and "house.") But at some time someone had the idea of forming these signs into independent entities, not as pictures or syllables, but as *letters*, which could be used to spell anything in any language.

But since the invention of the alphabet implies thousands of years of picture writing prior to such a breakthrough, one wonders whether the Phoenicians, under the pressure of recording the multiple transactions of their "overseas" commerce, suddenly invented it out of necessity, or did they get it or adapt it from some other older source? If this were the case, the Phoenicians as the principal navigators of very early times, would be the logical ones to uncover such an older source, if it did exist.

While it is generally accepted that the origin of the alphabet was at Byblos, Syria, where the oldest alphabetical writing has been located, relatively few ancient Phoenician inscriptions have been unearthed in Phoenicia compared to the profusion of them found throughout the Mediterranean, in Cyprus, Malta, Sicily, Sardinia, Greece, the coasts of France, Spain and North Africa, showing the spread of the Phoenician alphabet, not only in the Eastern Mediterranean, but in the western part as well.

The further west we go, of course, the nearer we are getting to the reputed location of Atlantis or at least of an advanced culture located past Gibraltar. The advanced but little known prehistoric civilization of southern Spain, including the lost city of Tartessos on the south-west Atlantic coast. Tartessos was reputed to have kept records for 6,000 years prior to its destruction, but has left us only a few "letters"—those on Schulten's ring, as well as some other inscriptions in Andalusia and North Africa which may or may not be connected. The indigenous white inhabitants of the Canary Islands possessed a system of writing when they were discovered in the fourteenth century that might have shown connections with the pre-Iberian Spanish alphabet, had it not vanished with them when they were decimated and subsequently absorbed.

The mysterious Etruscans, a cultured and artistic people living in Italy whom the Romans conquered and absorbed, have often been considered as a possible Atlantean remnant, especially since Plato said that they were once conquered by the Atlanteans ". . . they subjected parts of Europe as far as Tyrrhenia. . . ." Although the Etruscan alphabet, possibly derived from the Greek or Phoenician, can be read, we do not know how it sounded.

The Etruscans are mysterious because, except for tomb inscriptions, we have none of their literature or written records, which were destroyed, along with their cities, by the Romans. We know only from their tomb paintings (they painted the walls of their tombs as did the Egyptians, but more joyously) that they had a lively time while they lived. Several years ago three thin gold tablets were discovered in a ruin. Two of these have inscriptions in Etruscan and the third has a translation in Phoenician. However, as it turned out to be concerned with the dedication of a temple, the Etruscans, from a historical or place of origin viewpoint, remain as mysterious as ever. Still, the suggestion can be made that if Archaic Phoenician and Etruscan languages are related such relationship might point to a common, even older one, linked to the very origin of the true alphabet. At all events the inscription on the ring from Tartessos (as well as other pre-Roman Iberian inscriptions, seems to be written in the same alphabet, if not in the same language.

If any Etruscan records or literature are eventually found, one hopes that they will throw some light on the question of Etruscan origin and possible relationship with other cultures, Atlantean or Eastern.

Some similar hopes were held for the deciphering of the scripts of Minoan Crete labelled Linear A and Linear B. Minoan Crete, being a sea empire of a surprisingly advanced civilization in very early times, has often been associated with Atlantis and frequently proposed as the site of Atlantis itself, or reason for the Atlantean legend. When Linear B was broken by a young Englishman, Michael Ventris, shortly after World War II, no startling mysteries, other than the script itself, were cleared up. Some of the first material available for translation, for example, dealt in commercial transactions, accounts of estate administration, supplies and payments, and one account even detailed how much olive oil and perfume was allotted to slaves—an unusual comment on a sort of "welfare" slavery. Needless to say, hopes for more historically revealing information are being held for the eventual translation of the older script—Linear A.

During the long history of mankind tribes or races have developed writing or had writing taught to them and then, for various reasons, have forgotten it, as in the case of the Cretan scripts Linear A and B and the archaic Greek script of Greece itself. An unusual aspect of written Greek having disappeared from the twelfth century B.C. to about 850 B.C. and the emergence of a new script has been connected by James Mavor, an American archaeologist and oceanographer, in his recent *Voyage to Atlantis*, to a most intriguing section of Plato's "basic documents" when he refers to the reported conversation of the Egyptian priests with Solon in reference to written records which the Egyptians possessed but the Greeks did not, as ". . . (when) the stream of heaven . . . leaves only those of you who are destitute of letters . . . you have to begin all over again as children and know nothing of what happened in ancient times. . . ."

As written scripts are usually lost through the disappearance of a culture or collapse or takeover of one culture by another, the centuries long disappearance of Greek writing is somewhat of a mystery in itself, especially since the culture was continuous.

The Easter Island "alphabet," a series of curling lines and half pictures on wooden tablets, is an outstanding instance of a written

| | | | | | | | | |
|---|---|---|---|---|---|---|---|---|
| Indus Valley | | | | | | | | |
| Easter Island | | | | | | | | |
| Indus Valley | | | | | | | | |
| Easter Island | | | | | | | | |
| Indus Valley | | | | | | | | |
| Easter Island | | | | | | | | |

Comparison of examples of Indus Valley and Easter Island scripts, showing extraordinary similarity although the centers of their use were separated by thousands of miles.

language being lost when a culture deteriorates. Because of depopulation and conquest, the descendants of the people who wrote them knew they were writing but could not read them.

These tablets have not yet been translated and perhaps, until a key or translatable cross reference has been found, never will be. This Easter Island script, however, shows a surprising resemblance to the Indus Valley script used in the large cities of Mohenjo Daro and Harappa more than 5,000 years ago in what is now Pakistan. A comparison of the Easter Island and Indus Valley scripts offers rather convincing visual evidence that they are related but, since the Indus Valley script has not been deciphered either, the mystery of their relationship and their meaning is as deep as ever.

In fact it is even deeper for, if Easter Island was settled from the American continent as Heyerdahl has assumed, because of the direction of the flow of the Pacific current, then perhaps a form of the Easter Island writing went to the Indian Peninsula from America. Otherwise the appearance of this Indus Valley script would indicate that an ancient civilization had crossed thousands of miles across the open Pacific Ocean to establish a colony on a small island which is more a part or North America than of Asia. In addition, the ruins that still exist on Easter Island definitely resemble those of the coastal culture of Peru. A third possibility has long been considered: that Easter Island is a remnant of a Pacific lost continent, although examination of the floor of the Pacific Ocean has not sustained this theory.

In any case, whether the Easter Island writing came from the east or from the west, its similarity to that of an ancient Indian script constitutes a remarkable written language link between the Old and New Worlds across the Pacific, albiet in languages which cannot be read or even identified.

An example of the written language of a people being different from the spoken language exists in the case of the Tuaregs, the so-called "Blue People" of the Sahara desert as the blue dye they use in their protective veils tends to color their faces blue. The Tuaregs are thought to have language connections with Punic and Old Libyan, taking us back again to the Phoenician culture. But their alphabetical written language, T'ifinagh, which is *not* their spoken language, Temajegh, is being forgotten before it can be either properly classified or translated. This strange alphabetical script, lost in the desert, constitutes still another linguistic mystery —this time complete with "Atlantean" overtones.

In the Americas we have constant references to writing being introduced by gods or teachers coming from the east or from the Eastern Sea. Quetzalcoatl, for example, is referred to as coming from the "Black and Red Land" which, by inference can be interpreted as the land of writing, as black and red were the Aztec colors principally used in their picture writing. (The "Black and Red Land" also fits in with Plato's description of the cities of Atlantis being built of black and red stone.)

An interesting picture of a priestly or scholarly group who brought writing to pre-Columbian Mexico has been left to us by Sahagún, a Spanish chronicler of the conquest of Mexico, who reports it from ancient sources:—"(They) came from across the water and landed near (Vera Cruz)—the wise old men who had all the writings—the books—the paintings."

A strange element in Peruvian historical tradition is reported by Fernando de Montesinos, a Spanish recorder of Inca history. According to "spoken" history, the Inca Huanacauri (of an earlier dynasty than the one ended by the conquistadores) was advised by priests of the sun that, if he wished to get rid of the plague that was devastating his empire, he should abolish writing and the plague would subsequently abate. He thereupon imposed the death penalty on writing, killed some disobedient writers, and writing as well as the plague, one presumes, vanished from his empire. How was all this remembered without written records? Through the use of human "recorders" who were selected to memorize Inca history and literature. In fact quite long poems in Quechua and even traditional plays such as *Ollantay* have been "remembered" through vocalization from Incaic times and have subsequently been written down and produced in the modern era. The population, produce and tribute records of the Inca Empire were kept by a system of large tassels of colored and knotted strings and it is possible that the memory trained recorders used these as a substitute for written records to jog their memories. The complete use of the *quipus* is not understood even today, and it is possible that some Inca knowledge is still available (but not offered) in Quechua or Aymará speaking villages high in the Andes.

So many written inscriptions in the New World have turned out to be the work of present day Indians, explorers or even pranksters, that researchers approach with extreme caution the many "ancient" inscriptions found in South America in Venezuela, Colombia and Brazil as well as on the west coast. Some of them appear to be written in Greek, some in Phoenician, while others are indecipherable.

One must remember that large parts of South America are not only archaeologically unexplored, but are unexplored in any fashion whatever, except from the air, looking down on a thick jungle which appears much like a green ocean. This other ocean has been considered, partly because of inscriptions found along the river banks, which might have been harbors, and hills which might be ruins, and legends of lost cities under the blanket of trees, to be another possible key to Atlantis and pre-history, notably by the explorer Fawcett, who lost his life there, while seeking traces of the alleged "lost cities."

Although many of the inscriptions found in Eastern South America have been labelled hoaxes, it is unlikely that people wishing to perpetrate hoaxes would go so far up the river into the jungle to do so, or that the primitive jungle Indians would take the trouble to do so, or to learn Greek or Phoenician letters.

Moreover, certain concrete evidence seems to have been found of visits from across the ocean—a Roman coin cache, dug up in Venezuela, for example, with coins corresponding, at the latest date, to 350 A.D. As the jungle area is more completely explored, more inscriptions can be expected to be discovered and studied, giving us perhaps further indications not only about early American exploration but who the explorers were and what alphabets or writing systems they used.

Finally, we are left with certain linguistic memories, some possibilities of isolated survivals of a before-the-flood language, some undeciphered script whose future translation may clear up the mystery (or even make it more complex).

Linguistically, is there anything more? There is, and that element is the name of Atlantis itself. Supposing there was such a continent or empire, the name which the inhabitants called it may not have been the Greek or Platonian version. The constant appearance of the same letter sounds—A- T- L- N—in various languages for the name given to the point of race origin, the ancient homeland, the earthly paradise, the origin of culture, by peoples on both sides of the Atlantic *and beyond*, constitute a vivid reminder of a land and civilization that, whether it existed or not, mankind has been unable to forget.

# 11 ⛵ *Where Was Atlantis?*

Just as there is considerable divergence of opinion in the academic world as to whether Atlantis ever existed or not, even among its most fervent supporters there is a considerable difference of opinion about where it once was—and, presumably, still is. Many investigators think it is under the Atlantic, where Plato said it was. Others think it is under land—the sands of the Sahara, once an inland sea. Some others think it is under the Arctic ice, or under a number of other seas and oceans, while still others are of the opinion that Atlantis was simply a name given by Plato to another historic culture, and so placed "beyond the Pillars of Hercules" by geographical error.

While several thousand books have been written to prove or disprove the existence of Atlantis, it is interesting to check the most outstanding writers or investigators on the subject, ancient and modern, to see what the prevailing opinion is, or has been, on the location of Atlantis. Taking a sample poll of 270 authorities we come up with opinions as follows. (Considering the number of people who have written about Atlantis, only the most historically important or most outstanding investigators or actual expeditions for researching a special area have been counted.)

| Attributed Location of Atlantis | Number of Authorities Holding Opinion |
|---|---|
| A sunken island or land bridges in the Atlantic | 97 |
| It never existed geographically— only as a legend | 46 |
| North or South America—or both together | 21 |
| Morrocco or North Africa (including Carthage) | 15 |
| The Holy Land including Israel & Lebanon | 9 |
| Tartessos & Southern Spain | 9 |
| Crete and/or Thera | 9 |
| Gibraltar | 6 |
| Other islands in the Mediterranean and/or Malta | 6 |

| Attributed Location of Atlantis—cont'd | Number of Authorities Holding Opinion—cont'd |
|---|---|
| Sunken Continent in Pacific Ocean | 4 |
| Sahara Desert | 3 |
| Iran | 3 |
| Canary Islands | 2 |
| Ceylon | 2 |
| Mexico | 2 |
| Greenland | 2 |
| South Africa | 2 |
| Crimea & Southern Russia | 2 |
| Netherlands | 2 |
| Caucasus Mountains | 2 |
| Brazil | 2 |
| Nigeria | 2 |
| Arabia | 1 |
| Belgium | 1 |

| Attributed Location of Atlantis—cont'd | Number of Authorities Holding Opinion—cont'd |
|---|---|
| Britain | 1 |
| Catalonia | 1 |
| East Prussia | 1 |
| Ethiopia | 1 |
| France | 1 |
| Iraq | 1 |
| Mecklenberg, Germany | 1 |
| Northern Europe | 1 |
| Northern Polar Continent | 1 |
| Portugal | 1 |
| Siberia | 1 |
| Spitzbergen | 1 |
| Sweden | 1 |
| Venezuela | 1 |
| West Indies | 1 |
| Sunken island in Indian Ocean | 1 |

In the above listing no separate mention has been made of the Azores Islands since they are generally considered, by writers who place Atlantis as a sunken continent in the Atlantic, to be the topmost unsubmerged mountain peaks of the lost or "eighth" continent, as Atlantis is sometimes called.

In considering the above list, one is struck by the fact that almost a fifth of the investigators (who spent an unknown aggregate of years researching the subject) have come to the conclusion that Atlantis never existed at all, except in the minds of those who wrote about it. Many of these writers have felt that Plato either invented Atlantis as an object lesson to be used in his philosophical concept of the perfect state, or that he perhaps had heard the name brought back by travelers from the western Mediterranean and had used it in combination with existing places he had heard about whose advanced organization, as well as architectural and engineering feats would impress his listeners. Reports of the Greatness of Babylon, Crete or Persia could be fitted into this account of a "super power." Others have suggested that the Egyptian priests *may have* told Solon something of the sort that Plato reported, but did it with a view of gaining his goodwill and "building up" the Athenians as having been strong enough in the past to vanquish an Atlantean army.

Modern critics of the Atlantis theory seem to have softened somewhat since the days of Aristotle. This apparent sympathy with the subject even on the part of the doubters may have been brought on by the spell of the Atlantean legend, or because, with increased knowledge of the past, there is a general realization that certain prehistoric cultures have not been recognized for what they were, and that man's prehistory is older than we think. Some of the anti-Atlanteans have come to the conclusion that Atlantis fills a psychological need—the need of mankind to find refuge in the idea that once in a Golden Age things were better, before other factors destroyed man's first perfect civilization.

Others find it a useful object lesson, especially in view of the legend that Atlantis was destroyed by the moral deterioration of her people. In this they are joined by the believers in Atlantis of yesterday and especially of today, who hope mankind will heed the Atlantean lesson and not cause his own destruction a second time. Sooner or later the question of Atlantis comes to mind every time a mysterious or previously "unconnected" civilization is discovered; either when someone asks—"Could this be Atlantis?" or—"Is this what may have caused the Atlantis legend?" Several of these theories are particularly interesting because of the measurements involved; that is, taking the actual dimensions that Plato ascribed to Atlantis and to its capital city with its canal network and applying or interpreting them to several actual archaeological sites.

Albert Hermann, a German geographical historian among those who thought Atlantis was in Tunisia, based a great part of his theory on a possible mistranslation of what the Egyptian priests of Saïs told Solon. He notes that all measurements given by Plato are divisible by 30 and he therefore thinks that the Egyptian measurements were probably given in "schomos"—1 stadium equals 30 schomos—and that somehow, in a confused attempt to make the translation come out right, the interpreter *multiplied* the figures given him by 30. But we don't know whether Solon used an interpreter or not, as it is possible that the Egyptian priests spoke Greek. In any case, Hermann made Tunisia neatly conform with the measurements given for Atlantis, and in measuring the great central plain found that it too, when its dimensions are divided by 30, corresponds to that mentioned by Plato. In his opinion the

Shott el Djerid, a marshy lake where nearby digging produced sea molluscs, was formerly Lake Tritonis, an inland sea opening into the Mediterranean, and the huge circular canals were only 10 feet wide. Hermann thought he had located remains of the city of Poseidon, which he also connected with Arab legends of the ancient "City of Brass" in the Sahara, near the village of Rhelissia, consisting of only 15 houses but which happened to have some underground waterways (remnants of canals?). However, although the horizontal measurements offered by Hermann are at least debatable, an application of the vertical ones at the ratio of 30 to 1 would turn the towering mountains and lofty temples described by Plato into hillocks and huts.

Another German, a pastor named Jürgen Spanuth, presented a theory in a book published in 1953 placing Atlantis in the North Sea, at the mouth of the Elbe River, east of Heligoland, where reports of submerged buildings had long been current. Atlantis, in his theory, was the capital of a northern empire, the origin of the attack on Egypt as reported in Egyptian records in the twelfth century b.c. Concentrating his attention on some large rocks on the flat bottom which he thought might be the Atlantean citadel, Spanuth introduced a new element in underwater research—scuba divers. This was the first time, as far as we know, that divers have been used in the search for Atlantis, a development in Atlantean research both logical and promising for the future. However, in the case of the Spanuth divers excited telephone calls from the bottom to the mother ship from a depth of only about 26 feet indicated a certain over-enthusiasm. The divers reported finding a series of parallel walls, "made of huge rocks" whose subsequent measurements and even color fit in with Plato's account, although, like Hermann's theory, on a reduced scale. Two other diving expeditions on this site have made further measurements and brought up some pieces of worked flint.

Because of the general rise of the water level relative to the sinking of the coastline of large parts of Europe in the Stone Age and the Bronze Age many more sunken lands near the sea coast may offer further Stone Age finds. But diving near the shore in the north Sea or the North Atlantic is difficult and often unrewarding because of the lack of visibility, so different from the usually clear waters of the Mediterranean, Caribbean and other more southern seas.

Probably the most credible explanation of Atlantis as a present archaeological site of the island of Thera, in the Aegean Sea, is offered by the theory of Doctor Spiridon Marinatos, a Greek archaeologist, and Dr. Angelos Galanopoulos, a seismologist, which is the subject of a recent book *Voyage to Atlantis,* by the American archaeologist and oceanographer James Mavor. This theory explains the mysterious collapse of the Minoan Empire of Crete and the destruction of its splendid capital city of Cnossos by a volcanic explosion which tore apart the island of Thera in 1500 B.C., leaving a huge underwater abyss where part of the island used to be. This shock, it is thought, affected Crete as well, shaking down and burning its cities which never quite recovered their previous high civilization. Tidal waves from this shock must have crashed over shores all over the Mediterranean and engulfed coastal cities and towns, giving birth, perhaps, to some of the legends of a universal flood. Excavations have shown the presence of volcanic ash on Thera and Crete, sometimes over 130 feet deep. Future land or underwater excavations will undoubtedly give more information about such a catastrophe.

As Egyptian trade with Crete was interrupted by the mysterious decline of Cnossus and the Minoan Empire, perhaps the Egyptians, hearing no more of Crete, may have originated the legend that it had disappeared or sunk. It has also been suggested that the reports of a sea invasion of Egypt from the north may be a result of waves of people, dispossessed by the earthquake, attacking Egypt in an attempt to find new lands to settle in.

Dr. Galanopoulos further reinforces the Thera theory of Atlantis by dividing not only Plato's measures of distance, but also his other calculations by 10 if they are *over* 1000 but accepting them, for purposes of measuring Thera or Crete, if they are *under* 1000. In this way the surrounding moat of the central city of Atlantis, converted to miles, would not be 1100 miles around but 110 miles, which would be roughly the circumferance of the Plain of Messara in Crete. In like manner, the Atlantean army would be calculated at 120,000 men instead of 1,200,000 and the fleet would be reduced from 1200 ships to a more modest 120. Even the date given by Plato for the destruction of Atlantis would, if divided by 10, more closely conform to the actual destruction of Thera. A suggested explanation for this apparent discrepancy in numbers over 1000 is that the basic error was made in the translation of the Egyptian hieroglyphics or a misinterpretation of the Cretan script.

Arthur Clark, an outstanding science and science fiction writer, whose interests extend back into the past and into the depths as well as toward the future and into space, is of the opinion that, *even if Atlantis had existed,* the Mediterranean peoples would have remembered the Thera disaster as being more recent. He points out that no one talks about the San Francisco earthquake of 1836 because people remember only the more recent disaster—the "fire" of 1906—which was, incidentally, much less severe. Clark makes a further rather disquieting analogy: That, if an atom bomb were dropped in Chicago, survivors would remember only the bomb and *not* the Chicago fire of 1871.

Ignatius Donnelly had cited Thera (also called Santorini or Santorin), in 1882, as an example of the land changes of islands in the Mediterranean caused by volcanic eruptions and earthquakes and claimed that "a recent examination of these islands shows that the whole mass of Santorin has sunk, since its projection from the sea, over 1200 feet." Donnelly apparently referred to the deep "caldera" formerly occupied by part of Thera (Santorin) before it sank.

It is in the vicinity of this declivity that Dr. Galanopoulos, who has been involved in on-the-spot investigations, has suggested that the Atlantean capital was located, and has offered an ingenious superimposition showing how the citadel of Poseidon, as described by Plato, would fit within the north and south "prongs" of Thera which extend westward from the main eastern part of the island, forming a bay. Some underwater ruins have been reported at a depth of 120 feet in this bay.

The very aspect of Thera seems a remnant of some cataclysmic disaster with its smoking central cone, its black cliffs and its intermittent and frequent earthquakes, one of which recently demolished the funicular transportation to the central volcano. As a further proof of the area's seismic activity, small islands pushed up from the sea bottom appear from time to time, called by the local inhabitants "the burned islands." The water around them is so sulphurous that fishermen have found that they can clean their boats of barnacles by anchoring near the "burned islands" for a period of several days.

Thera's name is derived from the ancient Greek "wild beast," and Thera continues to live up to this suggestion of wildness and danger, as it rumbles and smokes, prepared at any time to give an "encore" of its great explosion.

But Thera and Crete are in the Mediterranean, definitely within the Pillars of Hercules, although Plato and legend put Atlantis out in the Atlantic. Could Plato or his sources have been geographically confused? Quite possibly, considering the epoch in which Plato lived. But still—the name Atlantis has not come up in connection with Thera or Crete—they were centers of civilization where catastrophies occurred. If we accept, as we must, considering the evidence at hand, the destruction of Thera, does this mean that we must abandon any thought of an Atlantic Atlantis? If we agree that Thera was Atlantis, then we still have to explain the name itself and certain puzzling and unanswered questions concerning traditions, racial memories and resemblances, the distribution of animals and peoples, the cultural similarities in art and architecture which were present on both sides of the Atlantic before Columbus.

But is there anything else? Are there any indications that Atlantis was not just a name given to a good story—based on a local disaster? There are some surprising things, which, when carefully considered in combination with other factors could do much to explain the mystery of Atlantis and open a path for even greater clarification in the future.

But before the obvious explanation (if any explanation of something that happened in the distant past could be obvious), let us have one further bit of mystery.

When the Canary Islands were discovered by Europeans in the fourteenth century, the inhabitants, once the Spaniards could communicate with them, expressed surprise that there were other people alive as they thought all humanity had perished in a catastrophe, but that some mountains, their present home, had remained above water. These islanders, moreover, possessed an odd mixture of a civilized culture and stone-age barbarism.

Among other things they had a system of an elective monarchy of ten kings (vide Atlantis), they worshipped the sun, had a special order of sacred priestesses dedicated to the sun, mummified their dead, built houses of closely fitted stone with walls colored red, white and black, as well as great circular fortifications, practiced a form of canal irrigation, performed tattooing by printing on their skins with seals, made pottery similar to that of the American Indians, made stone lamps, possessed literature and poetry and had a written *alphabetical* language. Their spoken language, now lost, seems to have been related to that of the Berber and perhaps also the Tuareg peoples of Africa, themselves often considered as possible racial survivors of Atlantis.

Several of the above cultural patterns agree closely with traditions of Atlantis and other Atlantic, Mediterranean or Transatlantic cultures. It has been suggested that the Canaries had been colonized by the Phoenicians; however, it is doubtful that a race of seafarers should have descendants who lived on islands but shunned the sea. This might be accounted for, however, if a flood or sinking had left a permanent mark on the psyche of the survivors.

Other indications point to considerable cultural deterioration, such as warfare being waged with stones and wooden weapons— but still with enough organization to hold out for some time against the Spanish.

A striking similarity in medical customs has been noted in the examination of the skulls of mummies. This is the technique of trepanning, of setting a gold or silver plate over the brain when the skull has been injured. Both the Guanches of the Canary Islands and the Incas of Peru practiced this delicate art, but one can only speculate on whether this stemmed from a shared Atlantean culture or whether it came as a natural development from peoples accustomed to clubbing their enemies over the head.

Even some of the physical features described in detail by Plato can be identified in the Atlantic Islands. Plato mentions black, white and red rocks, and volcanic rocks in these colors can still be seen in the stones of the Azores, the Canaries and other Atlantic islands. The mention of temperate climate and inexhaustable supplies of fruit still apply to Madeira, the Canaries and the Azores, while the great mountain rising from the central plain could be Mount Teyde, on Tenerife. Another coincidence can be noted regarding Plato's report of hot and cold springs, allegedly created by the trident of Poseidon. These springs, like the red, white and black stones, still exist in the Azores.

Paul le Cour—founder of the French organization "Friends of Atlantis" as well as an "Atlantis" periodical—visited the Azores and commented on these similarities and also on the present use of sledges in the Azores, which are hauled over round pebbles, a survival of a stone age transporting system which has come down to modern times. The Azores, in common with Thera but even more so, have the look of sunken lands about them, great black mountain peaks that rise directly from the sea.

In classical times there was evidently occasional contact between the Guanches and the Phoenicians, Carthaginians, Numidians and Romans, but the cultural level had retrogressed considerably before their "rediscovery" by the Spaniards.

There are no existing records relative to finding any indigenous inhabitants on the Azores, although some relics of either former inhabitants or seafaring visitors have been encountered. On the island of San Miguel a stone slab bearing an engraving of a building was discovered in a cavern. The visiting Paul le Cour, with an enthusiasm worthy of his position as founder of "Friends of Atlantis" classified this engraving as a representation of an Atlantean temple.

Apparently Carthaginians or Phoenicians visited the islands since Carthaginian coins have been found on Corvo, the most western of the Azores. The early explorers also found on Corvo a statue of a horseman made of stone, with an indecipherable inscription carved on the base. Unfortunately for subsequent investigators, however, the King of Portugal ordered it removed in the sixteenth century and it was inadvertently broken by the workers sent to remove it. The statue is gone and so is its base with the inscription. But one other fascinating item has come down to us, as reported by A. Braghine, a modern researcher, in his book *The Shadow of Atlantis*. When the Portuguese explorers, in search for new lands, first reached the Azores and saw the statue, they noted that the rider's arm was pointing due west—towards the New World. And the inhabitants of Corvo were reported to have called the statue *Catés*, which has no meaning in either Portuguese or Spanish but which, by an odd linguistic coincidence resembles, in the Quechua language of the ancient Inca Empire, the word for "follow" or "go that way"—*cati*.

In considering the Atlantic islands and their possible relationship to the shores of the Atlantic and, by extension, with the islands and coastal cultures of the early Mediterranean world we are getting very close to a possible solution of the mystery of Atlantis—a mystery that perhaps was never a mystery at all in that we have always had an evident explanation at hand.

Oceanography research, as well as a completely new field of investigation, underwater exploration by scuba divers, have united to give us a logical and believable answer.

Underwater explorers, visionaries though some of them may be, tend at the same time to have a practical and pragmatic outlook— it helps for survival. From first hand observation they have noticed, in recent years, that the waters of the earth have been rising through the centuries, and that is why there is still a fertile field for untouched archaeological discoveries along the shore lines of the Mediterranean and the Caribbean as well as other seas.

Jean Albert Foëx has offered the most likely and at the same time most obvious explanation of Atlantis in his recent book *Histoire Sous-Marine des Hommes*. This deduction is not based on legends or myths but on accepted scientific facts.

His deduction is based on the general agreement among geologists and oceanographers that, while the rise of the water level in the last several thousand years has been about a foot a century, a tremendous rise occurred several thousand years ago at a much more rapid rate. Around the tenth century B.C. the level of the sea was about 450 to 500 feet lower than it is now. The rise of the ocean level was due to the floods released by the melting of the last glaciers. When the third and last glaciation retreated and the ice melted the waters rose more than 500 feet, accompanied by rains and volcanic eruptions, especially in the volcanic zones of the Atlantic, which must have seemed like the end of the world in a great deluge. In other words, the Atlantean "culture complex," which could logically be expected to develop in pleasant temperate islands *and* adjacent shores, disappeared in the floodings and accompanying seismic disorders brought on by the melting of the last great glaciers. This rise in the water level could also account for the filling up or great increase in area of the Mediterranean Sea, the bottom of which is not a true sea bottom but is characterized by mountains and valleys.

This time, in our study of Atlantis, we are on generally firm scientific ground. We know that the glaciers existed—we know that pre-glacial man existed—and we know the rate of the ocean rise by radio carbon dating of materials dredged from the sea, including oyster shells, marine molluscs, peat, mastodon and mammoth remains and even prehistoric tools.

If we project the Atlantic islands as they then were—taking in all the surrounding sea bottom to a depth of 500 feet or more—we get islands with much greater land areas, not continents perhaps, but still big enough to support a numerous and industrious population, capable of developing a civilization. Also the other shores, those of France, Spain, Portugal, North Africa and America extended out as well, probably as far as the continental shelf, as evinced by the underwater canyons that lead from existing rivers to the edge of the abyss. These oceanic islands would not only be bigger than the present ones, but there would be more of them. This would also mean extensive dry land areas comprised of the great and little Bahama banks, where recent discoveries of underwater buildings and cities have been made. The "pre-flood" size of these areas and the Atlantic Islands reminds us of Plato's mention of ". . . other islands; and from the islands you might pass through the whole of the opposite continent . . ." The population centers of this prehistoric empire would be, of course, at the old water level, and it is here, as Foëx suggests, that the search for Atlantis should yield fruitful results: a search not for legends or traditions, but by exploring the very cities and ports of the engulfed

Atlantis. Underwater constructions, of unknown origin, have been reported both in the Azores and the Canary Islands.

With this explanation, seconded by science as far as the water levels are concerned, we bring Atlantis back into the Atlantic, precisely where Plato located it. But the Atlantic was different, somewhat smaller and containing much larger islands and nearer the coasts of the surrounding continents, just as Plato and others described it.

Even the time element is unexpectedly consistent. Plato gives the sinking of Atlantis as reported by the priests of Sais as about 11,250 years ago; while modern science gives 10,000 B.C. as the end of the last European glaciers, with subsequent flooding. The spread of Megalithic culture to Europe occurred around this time and as the dates for Tartessos, Southern Spain, North Africa and the Mediterranean Island cultures are constantly being dated further back they get consistently closer in time to the period of the last retreat of the glaciers and the supposed exodus from Atlantis.

In other words, it was all partially true—but somewhat changed in the swirling mist of legend and the inconstant memory of man. Once there were great islands in the Atlantic. Once there was a flood that seemed to cover the earth. But the flood waters did not recede. They are still with us. And the lands did not really sink but rather they were drowned. And, except for sections covered by coastal tides, they did not come up again. And the lost lands are still there, now deep below the sea, with only their topmost portions rearing their peaks over the Atlantic. And, along their submerged banks, the former fertile portions of their pre-deluge days, there must lie the ruins or the remains of their cities, palaces and temples.

The Atlantis suggested by this glacier-flooded Atlantic culture is, of course, hardly the world empire postulated by Donnelly, nor the golden age dreamed of by so many of its cultural descendants. It may or may not have been the supercivilization claimed by other writers, complete with modern and supra-modern inventions and punished for its sins as an example to us all. What *is* probable however, is that on fertile and fruitful islands certain of the Crô-Magnon peoples first developed a culture which they spread to other shores before and after the world changes that caused them to emigrate. We do not know what language they spoke and we have only a vague idea of their cultural patterns. But if we ever find out, and the chances of this are good, we will know a great deal more about the origin of our civilization, our cultural background, our prehistoric history and, perhaps, ourselves.

# 12 Where to Look for Atlantis

With the development of underwater exploration and archaeology, the question of finding Atlantis, with its cultural as well as material treasures, reverts to underwater research, certainly a most logical field of investigation in looking for sunken lands. Great advances have been made in scuba diving whose range and depth is constantly increasing and may, in the near future, with special combinations of gas mixtures, extend to 1200 or 1500 feet.

Deep dive submersibles, such as Picard's *Trieste II* and the French Navy's *Archimède* are capable of descending the deepest oceanic trenches. Other small submarines are being produced which are both extremely maneuverable and capable of action somewhat as if they were an extension of the diver's arms. In addition, they have sonar and TV facilities for underwater viewing. *The Alvin* (Union Carbide), a two-man submarine located and "rescued" the missing atom bomb off the Spanish coast.

Constant improvements are being made in the smaller models.

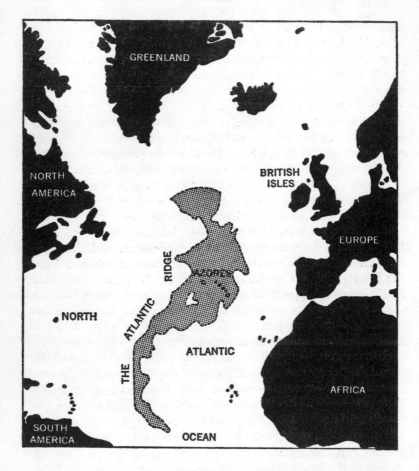

**Was this Atlantis?**
**High plateau along the Mid-Atlantic Ridge.**

The two man *Star Class I* of General Dynamics has an underwater limit of 6 hours and a 400 feet depth limit while the newer *Star Class III* can go to 3000 feet and has extended its dive period to 24 hours. Jaques Cousteau has perfected a diving saucer that can operate to a depth of 1000 feet and, for shallower depths, Dmitri Rebikoff's *Pegasus*, a sort of torpedo which a scuba diver rides like an underwater horse (steering it, like a good horseman, not with the hands, but the the the legs and flippers), combines mobility with optimum visibility. The *PX 15*, the *Ben Franklin*, which carries a crew of five, is an underwater vehicle used for prolonged research, with large view ports and the ability to stay underwater for weeks at a time, either operating under its own power or floating along with underwater currents at depths up to 2000 feet.

A special two-man submarine, the "Asherah" was constructed by General Dynamics specifically for underwater archaeological research in the Mediterranean connected with expeditions from the University of Pennsylvania. The "Asherah" makes a leisurely 2½ knots, is equipped with detection gear, closed circuit TV and stereoscopic cameras—a veritable custom made underwater archaeological research tool.

Another specially built submarine is planned for research into the "living" past, namely the tracking down of the Loch Ness monster, aided by direction of land and ship based sonar units.

Perhaps the most effective tool for scuba divers at great depths is the Link *Deep Diver* with its lockout chamber. Divers can be put in the chamber for compression prior to existing at a certain depth and then, on reentering the lockout chamber, can be decompressed, prior to coming back into the submersible; thus greatly increasing the depths to which they can descend and the dive time, as well as simplifying the problem of decompression.

The Sea-Lab project, now in the process of experimentation, enables divers to operate for long periods at a depth of more than 600 feet. It is especially interesting to consider that most of the Continental Shelf lies under less than 600 feet of water. The Sea-Lab, an underwater "house," rests on struts slightly above the bottom, with a direct exit to the sea in the floor, from which the water is held out by pressure, and through which divers, with Mark VII scuba rigs with special oxygen and helium mixtures, can exit directly to the sea floor. Divers are kept at the same pressure in the Sea-Lab as out of it and can therefore stay at great depths for long periods before being decompressed.

There now exists a system, used by submarines, of side-scan profile sonar, which can be used for locating underwater constructions as well as natural formations. An electronic investigation can even be made of underwater mounds to determine their composition. And through an amazing new technique, that of magnetic imprinting of the ocean floor, dating of underwater terrain can be accomplished directly from a submarine vehicle. Moreover, spectacular advances have been made in recent years towards the dating of artifacts, which now include, as well as radio carbon dating, the new techniques of thermo-luminescence and archeo-magnetism.

With such facilities at hand, locating some actual vestiges of Atlantis is certainly closer at hand than it was in the days when Wm. Gladstone tried to extract some funds for Atlantean research from the British Parliament or when Donnelly suggested that ". . . the nations of the earth may yet employ their idle navies (sic) in bringing to the light of day some of the relics of this buried people. Portions of the island lie but a few hundred fathoms beneath the sea; and if expeditions have been sent out from time to time in the past, to resurrect from the depths of the ocean sunken

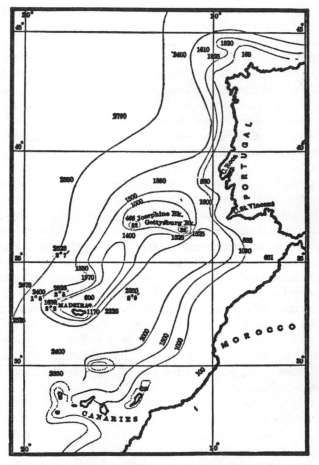

**Soundings around the Canary Islands and Madeira.**

treasureships . . . why should not an attempt be made to reach the buried wonders of Atlantis? . . ."

In effect, new diving techniques and submersibles have already brought complete exploration of the continental shelf within our range—and it is there that we will no doubt discover prehistoric remains and clues that will more conclusively settle the Atlantean "mystery." And not only in the vicinity of the Azores, Canaries and other Atlantic islands—for the scope of underwater exploration in the Atlantic and adjacent seas includes all the sunken lands that really did not sink at all, but that were covered by the rising waters of the last melting of the glaciers. This territory extends over a large part of the continental shelf of Europe and the Americas as well as the surrounding banks of the Atlantic islands, some of which may have been covered by rising waters which may have sunk due to seismic action caused by volcanoes.

These sunken lands, therefore, include many areas where Atlantis or other lost cities and, perhaps, continents, have previously been thought to have been located. The last settlements off the coasts of France, Spain and Ireland, the drowned lands of the Mediterranean basin, remains off the Baltic sea, the prehistoric cultural remains of North and Central America (including the "reappearing Atlantis" off Bimini), and especially the former lowlands and coastal cities of the Atlantic islands which, if they existed, would be near the old shore line or coastal plain, now, with flooding and sinking, at least 600 feet beneath the sea.

Therefore, the scope of Atlantean research may now extend all over the Atlantic littoral, as well as the Ocean islands and their submerged plateaus. But it is hardly to be expected that costly expeditions will be launched to find Atlantis, no matter how important or valuable the sunken remains and artifacts may be, without indications of specific locations in the other world which exists under the sea.

We can, however, expect archaeological finds relating to the Atlantean culture complex to be discovered on the ocean floor, mainly by chance, as with new and even more efficient equipment searchers engage in a variety of underwater investigation. This includes looking for lost ships, such as the atomic submarine *Scorpion*, which was finally located 400 miles southwest of Santa Maria, in the Azores; looking for oil or other materials on the continental shelf; mapping or studying the sea bottom; charting its underwater currents and observing the activities of its fish population.

The sea is the last great treasure house of the world and what has sunk or been engulfed in it is still there if we have the means to get to it and the ability to recognize it. Now, for the first time in the long history of the search for Atlantis, we have this ability. The key to our own past may lie at the bottom of the ocean.

A final question: Can Atlantis be found?

The near future will give us the answer. It can and will be—largely through the efforts of underwater explorers, the psychological descendants of the Atlanteans—the *new* "people of the sea."

# 13    *Has Atlantis Been Found?*

Since my researches in this area, more strange finds have given strong
indications that actual buildings dating from the times of Atlantis
may have been located on the sea bottom on the east and west sections and in the middle of the Atlantic Ocean. One must remember
that most concepts of Atlantis have been based on theories, legends,
historic references from antiquity, corroborative linguistic and cultural similarities that would otherwise be hard to explain, geological
and zoological coincidences and even psychic revelations and inherited memories. What then if some concrete evidence of underwater cities were actually found—in the very areas indicated by
Plato, and identified in popular belief since remote antiquity? Such
discoveries would necessitate a shift in historical perspective, a re-
evaluation of the progress of our own civilization and even, considering the time lapse between Atlantis and our own world, a
reassessment of the capabilities of what we usually call "primitive"
man. It could also be expected that the scientific establishment

would downgrade such finds, trying in each case to explain them away by some or any means to avoid, as Charles Hapgood has observed, "the horrid alternative of sunken continents".

This, in effect, is what has happened. Since 1968, when Dr Manson Valentine first discovered and explored the "Bimini Road", a sunken wall, foundation, road, or dock lying at a depth of about six fathoms east of North Bimini, scientific criticism has been immediate and severe. It has been suggested that these cyclopean blocks are really simple beach rock, broken off to look like blocks. It should be pointed out, however, that beach rock does not form great blocks which fit together in a pattern, that haphazardly splitting rock does not make 90-degree turns, nor does it normally have regularly laid-out passageways running between sections of it. Nor, above all, are "natural" beach rocks, lying on the ocean floor, likely to be found supported by stone pillars precisely placed beneath them! Anyone who has personally observed this superb stonework from underwater, stretching in a straight line thousands of feet into the darkening violet distance until it falls again under the sand (and later reappears off other parts of Bimini as if part of a gigantic citadel), will be under no illusion that it is anything but man-made. The rock, moreover, is of different composition from that on the beach and may, in the opinion of Dr Valentine, be specially treated or even a composite. Further out off Bimini at a depth of about 100 feet, vertical walls and even a great arch have been observed by pilots of commercial passenger flights and private planes. Underwater pyramids or bases for pyramids have been sighted from distances varying from several miles offshore to a hundred miles at sea. About ten miles from the southernmost bight of Andros, great circular interrupted patterns of monolithic stones have been photographed on the ocean bottom, some in double and others in triple concentric circles, suggesting a sort of American "Stonehenge" as it may prove to be when properly investigated. Dozens of unusual architectural vestiges have been found in different places on the Bahama Banks, some of them suggested only by the bottom vegetation growing over stone formations buried under the sea bottom, which still trace straight lines and perfectly circular or rectangular forms such as do not occur in nature.

In the case of those finds within easy access of surface divers, dating tests have already been applied. While stones cannot be dated within "historic" dating periods as can organic matter, fossilized mangrove roots growing over the stones of the Bimini Road have given a date of 10,000 to 12,000 years, coincidental not only with the date given by Plato for the destruction of Atlantis, but also with the accepted geological date for the melting of the last glaciers.

Further man-made structures abound in the Caribbean and neighboring areas. When the water is clear and unruffled, causeways or roads can be seen along the coastal seabottom off eastern Yucatan and British Honduras, leaving the mainland and stretching out under the sea to points too deep to follow them. Underwater soundings also show a 100-mile wall on the sea bottom off Venezuela. Geologists have proclaimed this a natural feature, explaining that it is "too big" to be considered as man-made. This is also the scientists' explanation for a ten-mile wall on the bottom of the Atlantic off Cape Hatteras.

North of Cuba a submerged building complex covering over ten acres has been reported, and apparently explored with Russian assistance. The USSR has in fact evinced a considerable interest in Atlantean research, and this is likely to increase with new exploratory maneuvers of Russian submarines. A fairly recent Russian expedition off the Azores confirmed P. Termier's thesis concerning the *tachylite* (a type of lava which forms above water at atmospheric pressure) brought up during the incident of the broken Atlantic cable in 1898, when he argued that large areas around the Azores had been above sea level 15,000 years ago.

Most of the western Atlantic and Caribbean discoveries have occurred on the continental shelf at relatively shallow depths, that is from 30 to 150–200 feet. Discoveries have been made with increasing frequency since 1965–69, coincidentally the period during which Edgar Cayce predicted, before his death in 1945, that Atlantis would rise from the sea. Among several reasons why these discoveries were not noticed sooner—which include the rarity of absolute surface smoothness in the Atlantic, and the fact that until very recently neither regular air routes nor scuba divers visited this region, the outstanding one is simply that it never occurred to archaeologists to search for prehistoric ruins in waters off the Americas.

There are of course indications that even more impressive ruins and artifacts may lie deeper down. A dive made by the French submarine *Archimède* off the northern coast of Puerto Rico revealed flights of steps cut in the steep sides of the continental shelf off Andros at a much greater depth than the other finds. And while we do not know who cut the steps or built the structures, one thing is certain—they were not accomplished underwater.

What may or may not be an extraordinary coincidence, is the fact that these prehistoric remains lie within the much-discussed Bermuda Triangle, the ocean area between Bermuda, Eastern Florida and east of Puerto Rico (40° EL), where hundreds of aircraft, large ships and small boats have been disappearing with all hands and without trace over the past thirty years (and perhaps for decades earlier). Reported aspects of their disappearances involve spinning of compasses, instrument malfunction, radio and radar blackout, glowing fogs, and electronic drain. One among many of the suggested explanations for the electromagnetic anomalies presupposes that an advanced Atlantean civilization possessed laser power sources— gigantic crystals one or more of which, still functioning, may lie on the bottom of certain abysses such as the Tongue of the Ocean, an ill-omened area between Andros and the Exuma chain. Edgar Cayce reported, through his psychic readings, that the Atlanteans did indeed possess such power, describing laser operations in some detail several decades *before* laser became an actuality in modern technology.

If we suppose that we have discovered submerged portions of Atlantis in the vicinity of the Bahamas and the islands of the Caribbean, what of Plato's conventional Atlantis in the middle of the ocean? The Bahaman discoveries would not however change Plato's observations. Remember that he said: ". . . This power came forth out of the Atlantic Ocean, for in those days the Atlantic was navigable; and there was an island situated in front of the straits which you call the Columns of Heracles: the island was larger than Libya and Asia put together, and was the way to other islands, and from the islands you might pass through the whole of the opposite continent which surrounded the true ocean; for this sea which is within the Straits of Heracles is only a harbor, having a narrow entrance, but that other is a real sea, and the surrounding land may be most truly called a continent. . . ." We must admit that a most important part of what he reported has received unqualified scientific support in the discovery of the American continent, while proof of the remainder may soon be at hand.

Undersea sightings from aircraft of buildings and entire cities in the vicinity of the Azores was reported as far back as 1942, when air ferry pilots flying from Brazil to Dakar glimpsed what seemed to be a submerged city on the western slope of mountains in the Mid-Atlantic Ridge, of which the Azores are the highest peaks, just breaking the surface. Such random sightings occur only when the sun and surface tension attain optimum conditions for underwater sightings. Other sightings of submerged architectural remains of what was perhaps the central Atlantean area have been noted off Boa Vista Island in the Cap Verde Islands, off Fayal in the Azores, while non-submerged remains of buildings and cities, perhaps dating from Atlantean times, were found by the early Spanish conquerors of the Canary Islands. (It is to be remembered that the Guanches, the inhabitants of the Canaries when the Spanish arrived, and who had preserved traditions of a great civilization lost in the sea, were no longer capable of constructing anything more than simple huts.)

All along the continental shelves and coastal plains of the Atlantic we are beginning to find remains of what may be relics of Atlantis —or relics of those who survived the catastrophe. It is also evident that the waters that engulfed Atlantis, and the seismic forces that changed the crust of the earth, operated on a global level.

Along the coasts of Ireland, France, Spain, Portugal and North Africa legends tell of lost ports and sunken cities, while real roads and walls stretch out under the Atlantic. There are two types of Mediterranean underwater remains—the buildings that have sunk in shallow waters since historic times (2500 years), not more on the average than one foot per hundred years; and others, at another much deeper level going back 10,000 years and more, long before the recorded history of Egypt, Greece and Rome.

Evidences of this deeper level, perhaps inherited by civilized peoples at the time when the Mediterranean Sea was a series of inland lakes, have recently been found by scuba divers. A well built underwater wall 14 kilometers long was found off Morocco by a diver chasing a fish. Dr J. Thorne, investigating the ruins on top of an underwater mountain 120 feet below the surface, noted roads going still further down the mountain into the purple blackness, into unknown depths. Five miles out in the Mediterranean directly south of Marseilles, Jacques Mayol, a French diver, has explored a mile-long shoal, running at a depth of 60 to 120 feet, with vertical shafts, quarries and slag heaps lying outside the shafts—in other words, a man-worked mine from a period in man's development contemporary with the Crô-Magnon period.

In short, a great quantity of Atlantean architecture and artifacts lies today beneath the sea, in areas that were coastal plains or valleys before the sea level changed throughout the world. D. H. Lawrence paints a vivid word-picture of that earlier world in *The Plumed Serpent*. Describing a time when "the waters of the world were piled in stupendous glaciers . . . high, high upon the poles . . ." ". . . the great plains stretched away to the oceans, like Atlantis and the lost continent of Polynesia, so that the seas were only great lakes, and the soft dark-eyed people of that world could walk round the globe . . ."

Vestiges of Atlantean culture may today subsist also on land in unexpected places, waiting to be recognized. Enormous stone walls on mountain tops in Peru (with stones so closely fitted together that they appear to be welded) were a mystery to the conquering Spaniards as well as to the Incas, whose empire the Spaniards were invading. Tiahuanaco, an incredibly old city in Bolivia, was apparently built so long ago that prehistoric animals were casually depicted on the pottery used by its inhabitants. The enormous buildings erected at an elevation of 13,500 feet with walls ten feet thick and foundation stones of 200 tons were constructed with such exactness and knowledge of physics and astronomy that many investigators are convinced that the builders could not have been of this earth, but must have come from elsewhere.

Geological discoveries around Tiahuanaco, such as salt lines in the mountains, former corn fields under the frozen snow-line of the surrounding peaks, and sea shells along the shores of nearby Lake Titicaca, indicate that the city was not a mountain fastness but rather an ocean port, forced up to its present altitude at some time in the remote past (Posansky, an archaeologist specialized in this area, calculates 15,000 years ago) during the volcanic upheavals accompanying the melting of the glaciers.

As parts of the earth's crust folded, other cities in South America may have been precipitated into the ocean's abyss. A striking indication of this possibility is to be found in photographs taken in 1965 by Dr Robert Menzies, then of Duke University, from the research ship *Anton Bruun* at the bottom of the Milne-Edwards Deep off the coast of Peru. Sonar recordings taken in this area indicated unusual shapes along the floor of the ocean, which otherwise seemed to be a mud bottom. Photographs taken at a depth of 6,000 feet showed what were apparently upright massive pillars and walls, some of which seemed to have writing on them. As attempts were made to take additional pictures of this unusual formation, it was noted that although the position of the special camera was changed from its original location by undersea currents, it took further pictures of apparently artificially shaped rocks lying scattered on their sides— some in heaps as if they had toppled over, perhaps at the time that this mysterious city fell more than a mile under the sea. While this incident at present marks the greatest depth at which supposed ruins have been found on the ocean floor, it is not unlikely that future undersea explorations at equal and even greater depths will provide, perhaps within a relatively short space of time, definitive proof of a world-wide civilization whose once flourishing cities now lie under the oceans of the world.

It is only with our newly developed equipment, both for dating and undersea exploration, that Atlantis, or what we may call the Atlantean Empire, is now in the process of being discovered. Whether or not the prospect is pleasing to conventional historians or to the scientific establishment, ongoing research under the sea is assembling pieces of a puzzle, or rather a mosaic, that will soon be too definite to be ignored or denied—even if pleasantly familiar tables of time and culture have to be changed.

The observation Plato reported the Egyptian priests as having made to Solon at Saïs is as applicable to us as Plato meant it to be to his ancient audience (and we must remember that the ancient Greeks did not realize they were ancient, but thought themselves as "modern" as we ourselves do now). As reported by Plato, "one of the priests, of very great age" observed to the visiting Solon: ". . . . you Hellenes are but children . . . in mind you are all young; there is no old opinion handed down among you by ancient tradition, nor any science which is hoary with age. And I will tell you the reason of this: there have been, and there will be again, many destructions of mankind arising out of many causes . . ."

This realization, common among the peoples of antiquity, is still shared by their modern descendants—ourselves. It has been consciously and subconsciously preserved by legends, traditions, racial memories and, in our day, is being reinforced by increasingly frequent discoveries. There were indeed cultures before our own "time span" of 3500 B.C. to the present. One of these, doubtlessly the culture immediately preceding our own "antiquity", was the one we call Atlantis—whose very name, however uncertain, has left such a vibrant echo in the history of our world and over the ocean which recalls its name.

# Bibliography

*Atlantis: The Antediluvian World*, by Ignatius Donnelly. London, 1882.

*The History of Atlantis*, by Lewis Spence. London, 1926.

*The Broken Spears*, by Miguel León-Portilla. London, 1962.

*Libro de Las Atlántidas*, by A. Vivante & J. Imbelloni. Buenos Aires, 1939.

*The Alphabet*, by David Diringer. London, 1948.

*The Story of Atlantis*, by W. Scott Elliot. London, 1896.

*Lost Continents*, by L. Sprague De Camp. New York, 1954.

*The Shadow of Atlantis*, by Colonel A. Braghine. New York, 1940.

*La Atlántida*, by E. Morales. Buenos Aires, 1940.

*Atlantis in America*, by Lewis Spence. London, 1925.

*The Problem of Atlantis*, by Lewis Spence. London, 1924.

*Legendary Island of the Atlantic*, by William H. Babcock. New York, 1924.

*Les Paladins du Monde Occidental*, by L. Talbot. Tangiers, 1965.

*El Misterio de la Atlántida*, by Luis León de la Bara. Mexico, 1946.

*L'Atlantide*, by Dennis Saurat. Paris, 1954.

*Earth Changes*, by Edgar Cayce. Virginia Beach, 1959.

*Voyage to Atlantis*, by James Mavor, Jr. London, 1969.

*Lost Atlantis*, by James Bramwell. London, 1938.

*Diving into the Past*, by Hans Wolf Rackl. New York, 1968.

*An Ancient Greek Computer*, by Derek de S. Price. "Scientific American," 1959.

*Histoire Sous-Marine des Hommes*, by Jean-Albert Foëx. Paris, 1964.

*Pleistocene Ice Volumes and Sea Level Lowering*, by Donn, Farrand & Ewing. "Journal of Geology," 1962.

*35,000 Years of Sea Level*, by F. B. Sheperd. Los Angeles, 1963.

*Ancient Oyster Shells on the Atlantic Continental Shelf*, by Merril, Emery & Rubin. "Science," 1965.

*The Aztecs of Mexico*, by George C. Vaillant. London, 1950.

*Les Atlantes*, by Etiene-Felix Berlioux. Paris, 1883.

*L'Atlantide: Translation and Notations*, by Dr. F. Gidon. Paris, 1949.

*Manuscrit Troano*, by Charles-Etiene Brasseur de Bourbourg. Paris, 1889 .

*The Children of Mu*, by James Churchward. London, 1931.

*Un Continent Disparu*, by Roger Dévigne. Paris, 1924.

*Atlantis*, by L. M. Hosea. Cincinnati, 1875.

*Queen Móo and the Egyptian Sphinx*, by Augustus Le Plongeon. London, 1896.

*The Secret of the West*, by Dmitri Merejkowsky. London, 1933.

*Les Pays Légendaires*, by René Thévenin. Paris, 1946.

*The Origins of Continents and Oceans*, by Alfred Lothar Wegener. London, 1924.

*Tartessos*, by Adolph Schulten. Hamburg, 1922.

*How I Found the Lost Atlantis*, by Paul Schliemann. New York, 1912.

*Unsere Atlantischen Vorfahren*, by Rudolph Steiner. Berlin, 1928.

*Essai sur les Îles Fortunées et L'Antique Atlantide*, by Bory de St. Vincent. Paris, 1803.

*L'Atlantide a-t-elle Existé?* by Th. Moreaux. Paris, 1924.

*Sacred Mysteries Among the Mayas and the Quichas 11500 Years Ago*, by August le Plongeon. New York, 1886.

*Tartessos*, by Gustav Redslob. Hamburg, 1849.

*L'Atlantide*, by Pierre Termier. Monaco, 1913.

*Atlantis, die Urheimat der Arier*, by Carl Zschaetzsch. Berlin, 1922.

*Atlantis and the Giants*, by Denis Saurat. London, 1957.

*Built Before the Flood*, by H. S. Bellamy. London, 1947.

*Hommes et Civilisations Fantastiques*, by Serge Hutan. Paris, 1970.

*Secret of the Ages*, by Brinsley Le Poer Trench. London, 1974.

# ACKNOWLEDGMENTS

The author would like to express his deep appreciation to the following persons and organizations who have given pictures, information, criticism or other help in the preparation of this book. This acknowledgment in no way implies either approval or disapproval of the author's theories by the persons listed. List is in alphabetical order.

J. Trigg Adams, president, Marine Archaeology Research Society.
The Benicasa family, descendants of the XV-century cartographer.
José Maria Bensaúde, director, Agencia Maritima "Ocidente," Portugal. and the Azores.
Valerie Berlitz, artist, author.
Lt. Col. Norman Bonter, author, researcher.
Comissão Regional de Turismo dos Açores.
Adelaide de Mesnil, archaeological photographer.
Natalie Derujinsky, photographer.
George Demetrios Frangos, historian.
Charles Hughes, linguist, philologist.
The Hispanic Society of America.
Jacques Mayol, diver, explorer.
Dr Robert J. Menzies, author, oceanographer.
Kenneth G. Peters, historian.
Jim Richardson, pilot, diver, researcher.
Robert E. Silverberg, historian, author.
Howard van Smith, author, columnist, editor.
Jim Thorne, author, archaeologist, explorer, diver.
Carl Payne Tobey, astrologer, NEA columnist, author.
Dr. Manson Valentine, archaeologist, explorer, author.
Krishna Vempati, author, researcher.